Knitted Toys

Knitted Toys

21 easy-to-knit patterns for irresistible soft toys

F<small>IONA</small> M<small>c</small>T<small>AGUE</small>

NEW HOLLAND

For Lucy and Molly

First published in 2004 by
New Holland Publishers (UK) Ltd
London • Cape Town • Sydney • Auckland

Garfield House, 86–88 Edgware Road
London W2 2EA
United Kingdom
www.newhollandpublishers.com

80 McKenzie Street
Cape Town 8001
South Africa

Level 1, Unit 4, 14 Aquatic Drive
Frenchs Forest, NSW 2086
Australia

218 Lake Road
Northcote, Auckland
New Zealand

ISBN 1 84330 582 8

Senior Editor: **Clare Sayer**
Production: **Hazel Kirkman**
Designer: **Lisa Tai**
Photographer: **Shona Wood**
Illustrations: **Carrie Hill**
Charts: **Kuo Kang Chen**
Editorial Direction: **Rosemary Wilkinson**

10 9 8 7 6 5 4 3 2 1

Reproduction by Pica Digital PTE Ltd, Singapore
Printed and bound by Times Offset (M) Sdn Bhd,
   Malaysia

Contents

Introduction

My first memory of knitting was as a child on holiday in Scotland, visiting my grandmother. Using oddments of yarn, I knitted little teddies and made outfits for them and since then I have been hooked.

I have always been interested in art, textiles, fashion and knitwear which led me to do a course in Fashion and Textiles. I chose to do a collection specializing in knitwear and have not looked back since.

This book is a delightful collection of over 20 adorable designs for soft toys. Knitted in beautiful soft yarns, they will be cherished by babies, young children and adults alike. Knitted toys make wonderful gifts and will be appreciated so much more than some of the expensive and mass-produced toys in the shops. Some of the designs are delightfully simple, while others will appeal to more experienced knitters and a helpful "skill level" indicator will help you decide where to start. Each project has been beautifully photographed and includes all the information you need on measurements, materials and tension, as well as full knitting instructions. Close-up details of the toys help illustrate the patterns even further. There are some projects simple enough to encourage a child to knit, such as the striped scarf or knitted sweater for a favourite teddy bear – perhaps they could go on to knit the teddy itself.

Throughout this book a wonderful palette of quality yarns have been selected, including tweeds, kidsilk, merino pure wools and cottons. I've used a whole spectrum of colours, from bold, vibrant primary colours of bright orange, blue and green, to a more soft chalky pastel range of lilac, soft pink, and muted blue.

The bright yellow cuddly duck, or cute baby pink piglet will become a toddler's best friend. Dressing up the pale pink loveable rag dolls and colourful clown will give the older child hours of fun. A perfect gift for a favourite friend would be the pretty fairy, knitted in a soft white silk haze dress, and trimmed with a silver yarn to give an extra special finishing touch.

Full knitting and finishing instructions are provided in the techniques section of the book, along with diagrams and illustrations to help you master certain embroidery stitches used in the book.

I hope you have as much fun creating your own special toys, as much as I did designing them.

Basic information

KNITTED FABRICS

All knitted fabrics are made using just two basic stitches, knit and purl.

GARTER STITCH (g st)

This is often referred to as plain knitting because every row is made with the same stitch, either knit or purl. This produces a reversible fabric with raised horizontal ridges on both sides of the work. It is looser than stocking stitch. One of the advantages of garter stitch is that it does not curl.

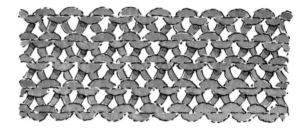

STOCKING STITCH (st st)

The most widely used knitted fabric. Alternate rows are knitted, the rest are purled. With the knit side as the right side it makes a flat, smooth surface that tends to curl at the edges. It needs finishing with bands, borders or hems.

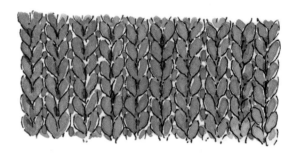

SINGLE RIB

Single rib is formed by alternating knit and purl stitches on each row to form columns of stitches. It produces an elastic fabric which is ideal for borders and neckbands. It is generally knitted on a smaller needle than the main fabric to keep it firm.

For an even number of stitches the pattern will be as follows:

*k1, p1, rep from * to end

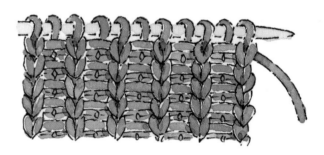

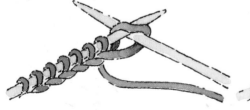

1 Knit the first stitch.

2 Bring the yarn through the needles to the front of the work and purl the next stitch.

3 Take the yarn through the needles to the back of the work and knit the next stitch.

Repeat steps 2 and 3 until all the stitches are on the right needle, ending with a purl stitch.

Turn the work and start again from step 1.

MOSS STITCH

This is a basic textured stitch. It is made up of alternating knit and purl stitches. Stitches that are knitted on one row will be knitted on the next row and stitches that are purled on one row will be purled on the following row. The fabric is firm and non curling, as well as reversible, making it ideal for collars and cuffs.

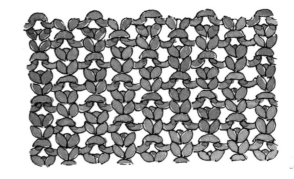

For an odd number of stitches, the instructions will be as follows:
Patt row: K1, * p1, k1, rep from * to end.
Repeat this row.

TENSION

Obtaining the correct tension/gauge is extremely important. It controls both the shape and size of an article, so any variations, however slight, can distort the finished look of the item. A tighter or looser tension will produce a smaller or larger toy than that shown in the photograph and if the tension is particularly loose, you may find that you have a very open fabric through which stuffing will show. Before starting a project, you are advised to knit a square in pattern and/or stocking stitch (depending on the pattern instruction) of perhaps 5–10 more stitches and 5–10 more rows than those given in the tension note. Place the finished square on a flat surface and measure the central area. If you have too many stitches to 10 cm (4 in), try again using thicker needles; if you have too few stitches to 10 cm (4 in), try again using finer needles. Once you have achieved the correct tension your garment will be knitted to the measurements given at the beginning of each pattern.

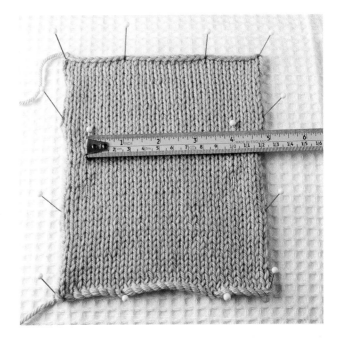

CHART NOTE

Some of the patterns in the book have charts. Each square on a chart represents a stitch and each line of squares a row of knitting. When working from the charts, read odd rows (K) from right to left and the even rows (P) from left to right, unless otherwise stated. Each colour used is given a different symbol or letter and these are shown in the key alongside the chart of each pattern.

☐ colour 1
  colour 2

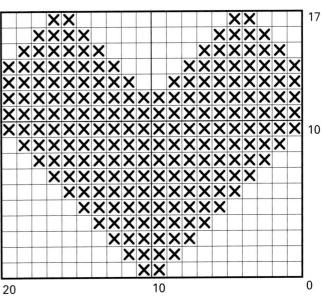

CHANGING COLOUR

There are two main methods of working colour into a knitted fabric: intarsia and Fair Isle techniques, but the projects in this book only use the first method. This produces a single thickness of fabric and is usually used where a colour is only required in a particular area of a row and does not form a repeating pattern across the row. The simplest way to do intarsia is to cut short lengths of yarn for each motif or block of colour used in a row. Then, joining in the various colours at the appropriate point on the row, link one colour to the next by twisting them around each other where they meet on the wrong side to avoid gaps. All ends can then either be darned along the colour join lines, as each motif is completed, or can be "knitted-in" to the fabric of the knitting as each colour is worked into the pattern. It is essential that the tension is noted for intarsia as this may vary from the stocking stitch if both are used in the same pattern.

PRESSING

Take a little time to press finished pieces before stitching them together, as this will help to match the edges accurately. After darning in all the ends, block each piece, except ribs, gently, using a warm iron over a damp cloth. Take special care to press the edges as this will make the sewing up both easier and neater. After sewing up, press seams and hems. Ribbed welts and neckbands and any areas of garter stitch should not be pressed.

FINISHING INSTRUCTIONS

When stitching the pieces together, match the colour patterns very carefully. Use a back stitch for all main knitting seams and an edge-to-edge stitch for all ribs unless otherwise stated.

EMBROIDERY STITCHES

FRENCH KNOT
Bring needle and thread out at the required position (A). Wind yarn round it twice. Turn, pulling twists lightly against needle. Insert back immediately next to the hole from which it emerged. Pull yarn through to back.

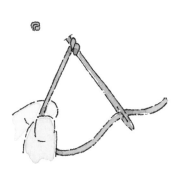

STEM STITCH
Bring needle out at A. Insert back at B and emerge at C [half way between A and B]. Continue in this way, making short, slightly angled overlapping stitches from left to right.

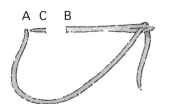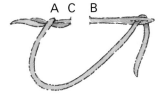

CHAIN STITCH
Bring the needle out at A, insert back at A and emerge at B, looping yarn under tip of needle. Pull yarn through to make the first loop. Continue in this way.

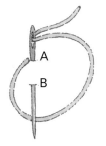

SATIN STITCH

Bring the needle out at A. Work stitches close together. Stitches can be made straight across or at an angle depending on the required finish. Care must be taken to keep a good edge, do not pull thread too tightly, or the knitting will be distorted.

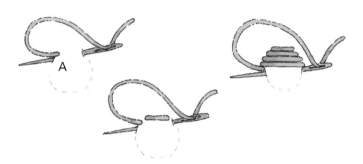

LAZY DAISY STITCH

Bring needle out at A. Insert back at A, and emerge at B, looping yarn under tip of needle. Pull needle through and over loop and insert at C. Emerge at D for next stitch.

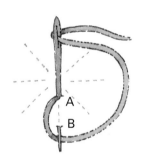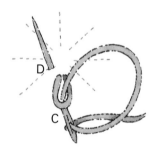

STAR STITCH

Bring needle out at A. Insert at B, and emerge at C, Insert needle at D, emerge at E, insert needle at F, thus completing the stitch.

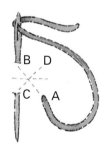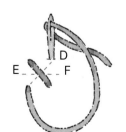

ADDITIONAL TECHNIQUES

CORDING

Cut the required number of strands of yarn 2 to 3
times the length of the finished cord. Knot together at
each end and attach one end to a hook. Insert a
knitting needle through the other end and turn
clockwise until the strands are tightly twisted.
Holding the cord in the centre, bring the two ends
together so that the two halves twist together. Knot
the cut ends together and trim.

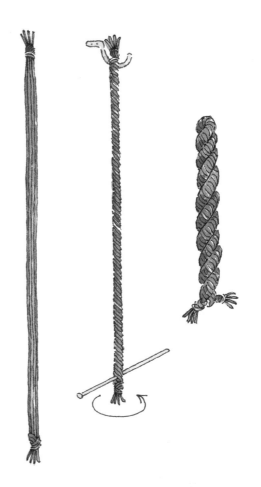

FRINGING

Cut the yarn into the required lengths. With the
wrong side of the fabric facing you, insert a crochet
hook from the front to the back, fold two strands in
half and place the loop on the hook. Pull the loop of
yarn through, then draw the ends through this loop
and pull the knot tight. Repeat at regular intervals.

KNITTING NEEDLE CONVERSION TABLE

Metric	British	American
2 mm	14	00
2¼ mm	13	1
2¾ mm	12	2
3 mm	11	2/3
3¼ mm	10	3
3¾ mm	9	5
4 mm	8	6
4½ mm	7	7
5 mm	6	8
5½ mm	5	8
6 mm	4	9
6½ mm	3	10
7 mm	2	10½
7½ mm	1	11
8 mm	0	12
9 mm	00	13
10 mm	000	15

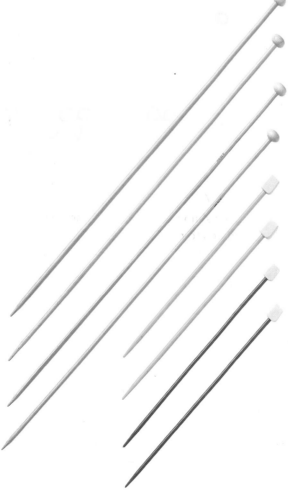

GLOSSARY OF UK/US TERMS

cast off = bind off
colour = shade
tension = gauge
knit up = pick up and knit
make up (garment) = finish (garment)
moss stitch = seed stitch
st st = stockinette st
yarn forward, yarn over needle or yarn round needle = yarn over.

ABBREVIATIONS

alt	alternate
beg	begin(ning)
cont	continue
ch	chain stitch (crochet)
dc	double crochet
dec	decreas(e)(ing)
foll	following
g st	garter stitch (k every row)
inc	increas(e)(ing)
k	knit
m1	make one by raised increasing
mm	millimetres
meas	measures
patt	pattern
p	purl
psso	pass slipped stitch over
rem	remain(ing)
rep	repeat
rev st st	reverse stocking stitch (RS row p, WS row k)
RS	right side
skpo	slip 1, knit 1, pass slipped stitch over
sl 1	slip one stitch
st(s)	stitch(es)
st st	stocking stitch (RS row k, WS row p)
tbl	through back of loop(s)
tog	together
WS	wrong side
yb	yarn back
yfwd	yarn forward
yon	yarn over needle
yrn	yarn round needle

YARNS

Patons Diploma Gold DK: a double-knitting yarn (55% wool, 25% acrylic, 20% nylon); approximately 120 m/131 yd per 50 g/1¾ oz ball.

Patons Diploma Gold 4 Ply: a 4 ply yarn (55% wool, 25% acrylic, 20% nylon); approximately 184 m/201 yd per 50 g/1¾ oz ball.

Rowan Handknit DK Cotton: a medium-weight cotton yarn (100% cotton); approximately 85 m/90 yd per 50 g/1¾ oz ball.

Rowan 4 Ply Cotton: a 4 ply cotton yarn (100% cotton); approximately 170 m/182 yd per 50 g/1¾ oz ball.

Rowan 4 Ply Soft: a 4 ply yarn (100% merino wool); aproximately 175 m/186 yd per 50 g/1¾ oz ball.

Rowan Kid Classic: a 70% lambswool, 26% kid mohair, 4% nylon yarn, approximately 140 m/151 yd per 50 g/1¾ oz ball.

Rowan Kidsilk Haze: a 70% super kid mohair, 30% silk yarn, approximately 210 m/229 yd per 25 g/1 oz ball.

Rowan Lurex Shimmer: an 80% viscose, 20% polyester yarn, approximately 95 m/103 yd per 25 g/1 oz ball.

Jaeger Baby Merino DK: a double-knitting yarn (100% merino); approximately 120 m/131 yd per 50 g/1¾ oz ball.

Jaeger Matchmaker Merino DK: a double-knitting wool yarn (100% merino wool); approximately 120 m/131 yd per 50 g/1¾ oz ball.

Jaeger Matchmaker Merino 4 Ply: a 4 ply yarn (100% merino wool); approximately 183 m/200 yd per 50 g/1¾ oz ball.

Jaeger Luxury Tweed: a 4 ply yarn (100% merino wool); approximately 180 m/199 yd per 50 g/1¾ oz ball.

Jaeger Shetland: a chunky yarn (80% wool, 20% alpaca); approximately 166 m/171 yd per 100 g/3½ oz ball.

CARE INSTRUCTIONS
Check on ball band for washing instructions.

STUFFING
Always use washable toy stuffing which conforms to safety standards to make up toy projects. Take care not to overstuff the toys as the fabric may stretch so that the stuffing shows through; likewise, understuffing can make the toy too limp.

SAFETY
When knitting toys for children, it is important to bear in mind the age of the child for whom it is intended. Never use buttons or plastic extras for eyes as they could easily come loose and be swallowed. In general, make sure that toys given to young children have all extras securely attached and sewn in place.

Ball with bell

This delightful ball is perfect for a newborn baby – the combination of bright colours, soft yarn and a gently tinkling bell sewn inside means it will provide lots of stimulation.

MEASUREMENTS
Height of ball approximately 12 cm (5 in)

MATERIALS
• Small amounts of Rowan Handknit DK Cotton (50 g balls) in Sunflower (A), Flame (B), Rosso (C), Diana (D), Oasis (E) and Gooseberry (F)
or
• Small amounts in Popcorn (A), Lupin (B), Flame (C), Gooseberry (D), Ice Water (E) and Pink (F)
• Pair of 3¼ mm (UK 10/US 3) knitting needles
• 1 toy bell
• Washable toy stuffing

ABBREVIATIONS
See page 14.

TENSION
24 sts and 32 rows to 10 cm (4 in) measured over stocking stitch using 3¼ mm (UK 10/US 3) needles.

FIRST SECTION
With 3¼ mm (UK 10/US 3) needles and A, cast on 1 st.
Knit into back and front of this st. (2 sts.)
Cont in A, work in st st, starting with a p row.
Inc into first and last st on next 2 rows.
Inc into first and last st on next 2 alt rows.
Inc into first and last st on foll 3rd row, twice. (14 sts.)
Work 3 rows straight.
Inc into first and last st on next row. (16 sts.)
Work 16 rows straight.
Dec 1 st at each end of next row. (14 sts.)
Work 5 rows straight.
Dec 1 st at each end of foll 3rd row, twice. (10 sts.)
Work 3 rows straight.
Dec 1 st at each end of next 2 alt rows.
Dec 1 st at each end of next 2 rows.
P 1 row. K2tog, and fasten off.
Repeat to make 5 more sections in the same way using colours B, C, D, E, F.

TO MAKE UP
Join sections neatly, leaving a small opening.
Insert the stuffing and bell and sew up the opening.

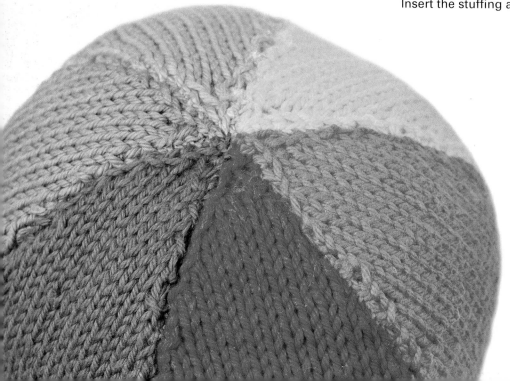

Penguin

Penguins are universally adored by children and adults alike. Who could resist this cuddly knitted version? The simple design means that he is perfect for a beginner knitter.

MEASUREMENTS
23 cm (9 in) tall

MATERIALS
• 1 x 50 g ball Patons Diploma Gold DK in Black (MC)
• Small amounts of White (A), Yellow (B), Orange (C) and Blue (D)
• Washable toy stuffing
• Pair of 3¼ mm (UK 10/US 3) knitting needles

ABBREVIATIONS
See page 14.

TENSION
24 sts and 32 rows to 10 cm (4 in) measured over stocking stitch using 3¼ mm (UK 10/US 3) needles.

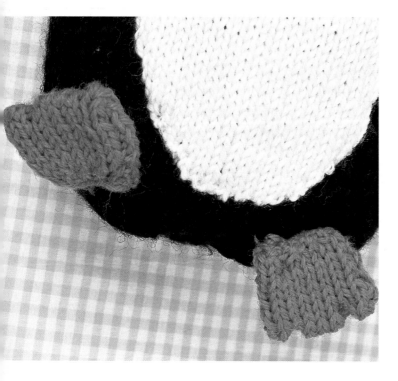

BODY
With 3¼ mm (UK 10/US 3) needles and MC, cast on 20 sts.
1st row: [WS] Purl to end.
2nd row: [RS] Inc in each st to end. (40 sts.)
Rep these 2 rows, once more. (80 sts.)
Cont straight until work meas 18 cm (7 in), ending with a WS row.
Next row: [RS] [K2tog] to end. (40 sts.)
Work 11 rows st st.
Next row: [RS] [K2tog] to end. (20 sts.) P 1 row. Rep last 2 rows once more. (10 sts.)
Break yarn, thread through rem sts, pull up and fasten off securely.

CHEST
With 3¼ mm (UK 10/US 3) needles and A, cast on 10 sts.
Work in st st and inc 1 st at each end of next 7 rows. (24 sts.)
Cont straight until work measures 10 cm (4 in).
Cont in st st, at the same time dec 1 st at each end of next 7 rows. (10 sts.) Cast off rem 10 sts.

FLIPPERS (make 2)
With 3¼ mm (UK 10/US 3) needles and MC, cast on 7 sts.
Work in g st and inc 1 st at each end of next 5 rows. (17 sts.)
Cont straight for 6 cm (2½ in).
Dec 1 st at each end of next 5 rows. (7 sts.)
Cast off.

FLIPPER LININGS (make 2)
With 3¼ mm (UK 10/US 3) needles and A, cast on 5 sts.
Work in st st and inc 1 st at each end of next 4 rows. (13 sts.)
Cont straight for 5.5 cm (2 in).
Dec 1 st at each end of next 4 rows. (5 sts.)

Cast off.
Sew each pair of flippers together, white to be on the inside of the black.

FEET (make 2)
With 3¼ mm (UK 10/US 3) needles and C, cast on 5 sts.
Next row: Inc in every st. (10 sts.)
Work in st st for 9 rows.
Next row: K1, [k2, yfwd, k2tog] twice, k1. (10 sts.)
Beg with a p row, work 8 rows in st st.
Next row: [P2tog] to end. (5 sts.) Cast off.
Fold in half, sew cast-on and cast-off edges together.

BEAK
With 3¼ mm (UK 10/US 3) needles and B, cast on 12 sts.

Work in st st and dec 1 st at each end of next 5 alt rows. (2 sts.)
K2tog. Fasten off.

TO MAKE UP
Join body seam neatly, and stuff firmly.
Fold wings in half and attach, with white side positioned next to body.
Slip stitch chest in position centrally on the front of penguin.
Embroider eyes with Blue in satin stitch as shown in photograph.
Join seam of beak, and attach to face, position between eyes and just below.
Sew feet to front of base, position with a gap in between.

Duck

This lovely duck will make a superb companion and is quite at home perched at the end of a bed or on a windowsill. The bright colours will appeal to younger children.

MEASUREMENTS
22 cm (8½ in) tall when seated

MATERIALS
- 1 x 50 g ball Patons Diploma Gold DK in Yellow (MC)
- Small amounts of Orange (A) and Black (B)
- Washable toy stuffing
- Polystyrene granules
- Pair of 3 mm (UK 11/US 2/3) knitting needles

ABBREVIATIONS
See page 14.

TENSION
26 sts and 36 rows to 10 cm (4 in) measured over stocking stitch using 3 mm (UK 11/US 2/3) needles. 26 sts and 42 rows to 10 cm (4 in) measured over garter stitch using 3 mm (UK 11/US 2/3) needles.

BODY BACK
With 3 mm (UK 11/US 2/3) needles and MC, cast on 46 sts.
1st row: [RS] Knit to end.
2nd row: [WS] Purl to end.
Work in st st for 30 rows.
Dec 1 st at each end of next and every foll alt row until 30 sts rem.
Dec 1 st at each end of every row until 20 sts rem.
Cast off.

BODY FRONT
With 3 mm (UK 11/US 2/3) needles and MC, cast on 36 sts.
1st row: [RS] Knit to end.
2nd row: [WS] Purl to end.
Work in st st for 30 rows.
Dec 1 st at each end of next and every foll 3rd row until 28 sts rem.
Dec 1 st at each end of 3rd and every foll alt row until 20 sts rem.
Work 1 row. Cast off.

BASE
With 3 mm (UK 11/US 2/3) needles and MC, cast on 36 sts.
Work in st st for 10 rows.
Dec 1 st at each end of next row.
Work 4 rows, dec 1 st at each end of next row.
Dec 1 st at each end of every alt row 3 times.
Dec 1 st at each end of every row until there are 18 sts. Cast off.

HEAD
With 3 mm (UK 11/US 2/3) needles and MC, cast on 30 sts.

1st row: [RS] Knit to end.

2nd row: [WS] Purl to end.

Next row: [Inc 1, k1] to end. (45 sts.)

P 1 row.

Next row: [K1, inc 1, k1] to end. (60 sts.)

Work in st st for 3 rows.

Next row: [K1, inc 1, k2] to end. (75 sts.)

Work in st st for 11 rows.

Shape face

Next row: K15, [k2tog, k1] 3 times, k27, [k2tog, k1] 3 times, k15. (69 sts.)

Work 1 row.

Next row: K15, [k2tog] 3 times, k27, [k2tog] 3 times, k15. (63 sts.)

Work in st st for 9 rows.

Next row: [K1, k2tog] to end. (42 sts.)

Next row: [K1, k2tog] to end. (28 sts.)

Next row: [K2tog] to end. (14 sts.)

Break yarn, thread through rem sts, pull up and fasten off securely.

ARMS [make 4]

With 3 mm (UK 11/US 2/3) needles and MC, cast on 10 sts.

1st row: [RS] Knit to end.

2nd row: [WS] Purl to end. Working in st st throughout, inc 1 st at each end of every row until there are 16 sts.

Work straight for 2 rows.

Inc 1 st at each end of next row.

Work 5 rows.

Dec 1 st at each end of every alt row until there are 10 sts.

Work straight for 22 rows.

Cast off rem sts.

LEGS [make 2]

With 3 mm (UK 11/US 2/3) needles and A, cast on 20 sts.

Work in g st until work meas 9 cm (3½ in).

Cast off.

FEET [make 4]

With 3 mm (UK 11/US 2/3) needles and A, cast on 10 sts.

Work in g st throughout. Inc 1 st at each end of every 3rd row until there are 24 sts.

Shape Front

Next row: K8, turn and work on these sts only. Dec 1 st at each end on next and foll alt row. (4 sts.)

Work 1 row.

Cast off.

Rejoin yarn to rem 16 sts.

K8. Turn and work on these sts only.

Dec 1 st at each end on next and foll alt row. (4 sts.)

Work 1 row. Cast off.

Rejoin yarn to rem 8 sts.

K 1 row.

Dec 1 st at each end of next and alt row. (4 sts.)

Work 1 row.

Cast off.

BEAK [make 2]

With 3 mm (UK 11/US 2/3) needles and A, cast on 8 sts.

Work in g st throughout.

Next row: Inc 1 st, k to end.

Rep last row until there are 18 sts. Work 8 rows straight.

Cast off.

TO MAKE UP

Join each leg seam.

Sew feet pieces together, leaving top edge open.

Stuff legs and feet quite firmly with toy stuffing.

Sew cast-on edges of legs on to foot, centrally.

Sew cast-off edges of legs to body, leaving a gap of 4 cm (1½ in) in between.

Join body seam neatly leaving neck edge open.

Stuff body with toy stuffing.

Join head seam, leaving neck edge open, then stuff firmly with toy stuffing.

Place together head and body seams, and join together along neck edge.

The head seam runs down centre back.

Join arms pieces together.

Leaving top edge open, fill lightly with polystyrene granules.

Position arms to top of body side seams as shown on photograph.

Join beak pieces, leaving top edge open and stuff firmly with toy stuffing.

Position and attach to face.

Embroider eyes in Black using satin stitch. Make sure they are evenly spaced above the beak.

Bugs

These charming knitted bugs with their smiling faces are
perfect for hanging over a pram or cot. Alternatively, you
could make them into a mobile for the nursery.

SKILL LEVEL 1

MEASUREMENTS
6 cm (2¼ in) long

MATERIALS
• Oddments of Patons Diploma Gold 4 ply in Black,
  Yellow, Green, Pink, Red, Blue, Violet.
• Small amount washable toy stuffing
• Pair of 2¾ mm (UK 12/US 2) knitting needles

ABBREVIATIONS
See page 14.

TENSION
30 sts and 38 rows to 10 cm (4 in) measured over
stocking stitch using 2¾ mm (UK 12/US 2) needles.

BEE
BODY
With 2¾ mm (UK 12/US 2) needles and Black, cast on
6 sts.
Next row: Inc in each st knitwise. (12 sts.)
Next row: Inc in each st purlwise. (24 sts.)
Join in Yellow, working in stripes of 2 rows Yellow,
2 rows Black, cont as follows:
1st row: Knit to end.
2nd row: K1, p22, k1.
Rep these last 2 rows 8 more times. (18 rows.)
Break off Black and join in Pink.
Work 8 rows st st.
Next row: [K2tog] to end. (12 sts.)
Next row: [P2tog] to end. (6 sts.)
Break yarn, thread through rem sts, pull up tightly
and fasten off securely.

LEGS (make 6)
With 2¾mm (UK 12/US 2) needles and Black, cast on
4 sts and work in st st for 10 rows. Cast off.

ANTENNAE (make 2)
**With 2¾ mm (UK 12/US 2) needles and Yellow, cast
on 1 st.
Make bobble as follows:
[k1, p1, k1] all into next st, turn, p3, turn, k3, turn,
p3tog, pull up and fasten off, forming a bobble. **
***With black, cast on 4 sts. Work 4 rows st st.
Cast off.
Roll along from cast-on edge to cast-off edge and
stitch along edge.
Sew bobble in place to top of antenna.***

WINGS (make 2)
With 2¾ mm (UK 12/US 2) needles and Black, cast on
5 sts.
Next row: Inc in every st. (10 sts.)
Knit every row for 15 rows.
Break yarn, thread through rem sts, pull up tightly
and fasten off securely.

TO MAKE UP
Join body seam neatly, leaving a small opening. Stuff
body, then stitch up small opening.
Sew the gathered edges of wings to the top of the
body as in photograph.
With Black, make a tightly twisted cord loop (see
page 13) and stitch in between the wings.
Stitch side seams of legs and stitch to under side of
body.
Work a few satin stitches in Red for nose, French knot
in Black for eyes, stem stitch in Black for mouth.
Attach the antennae behind the eyes.

BLUE BUG
BODY
With 2¾ mm (UK 12/US 2) needles and Blue, cast on 6 sts.

Next row: Inc in each st knitwise. (12 sts.)

Next row: Inc in each st purlwise. (24 sts.)

Work 2 rows Blue, then join in Violet, working in stripes as follows:

2 rows Violet, 4 rows Blue.

1st row: Knit to end.

2nd row: Purl to end.

Rep these last 6 rows twice more. (18 rows.)

Work 2 rows Violet.

Break off Violet, and join in Pink.

Work 8 rows st st.

Next row: [K2tog] to end. (12 sts.)

Next row: [P2tog] to end. (6 sts.)

Break yarn, thread through rem sts, pull up tightly and fasten off securely.

LEGS (make 6)
With 2¾ mm (UK 12/US 2) needles and Violet, cast on 4 sts and work in st st for 10 rows. Cast off.

ANTENNAE (make 2)
With Violet, make bobble as for Bee from ** to **.
With Blue, make antennae as for Bee from *** to ***.

WINGS
With Violet, work as for Bee wings.

TO MAKE UP
With Violet, make cord, and complete make up as for Bee.

LADYBIRD
BODY
With 2¾ mm (UK 12/US 2) needles and Red, cast on 6 sts.

Next row: Inc in each st knitwise. (12 sts.)

Next row: Inc in each st purlwise. (24 sts.)

Work in st st for 18 rows.

Break off Red, and join in Pink.

Work 8 rows st st.

Next row: [K2tog] to end. (12 sts.)

Next row: [P2tog] to end. (6 sts.)

Break yarn, thread through rem sts, pull up tightly

and fasten off securely.
For legs, wings and cord work as set for Bee.

ANTENNAE (make 2)

With Red, make bobble as for Bee from ** to **.
With Black, make antennae as for Bee from *** to
***.

TO MAKE UP

With Black, satin stitch black spots on red body.
Complete make up as for Bee.

GREENFLY

BODY

With 2¾ mm (UK 12/US 2) needles and Green, cast on
6 sts.
Next row: Inc in each st knitwise. (12 sts.)
Next row: Inc in each st purlwise. (24 sts.)
Work 2 rows Green, then join in Violet, working in
stripe as follows:
4 rows Violet, 4 rows Green.
Rep these last 8 rows twice. (16 rows.)
Break off Green. Join in Pink, work 8 rows st st.

△ Thread the bugs on to a length of yarn to hang over a pram.

Next row: [K2tog] to end. (12 sts.)
Next row: [P2tog] to end. (6 sts.)
Break yarn, thread through rem sts, pull up tightly
and fasten off securely.

LEGS (make 6)

With 2¾ mm (UK 12/US 2) needles and Green, cast on
4 sts and work in st st for 10 rows. Cast off.

ANTENNAE (make 2)

With Yellow, make bobble as for Bee from ** to **.
With Green, make antennae as for Bee from *** to
***.

WINGS

With Green, work as for Bee wings.

TO MAKE UP

With Green, make cord, and complete make up as for
Bee.

Farm animal finger puppets

Children love farmyard animals and these delightful finger puppets will provide endless amusement. Choose from a rabbit, cow, pig, mouse or lamb – or knit the whole set!

SKILL LEVEL 1

MEASUREMENTS
8 cm (3 in) tall

MATERIALS
• Oddments of Jaeger Matchmaker Merino 4 ply in White (A), Black (B), Oatmeal (C), Pink (D), and Grey (E).
• Oddments of Jaeger Luxury Tweed in Pebble (F)
• Oddments of dark pink embroidery thread
• Small amount washable toy stuffing
• Pair of 2¾ mm (UK 12/US 2) knitting needles
• Pair of 2¾ mm (UK 12/US 2) double pointed knitting needles

ABBREVIATIONS
See page 14.

TENSION
30 sts and 38 rows to 10 cm (4 in) measured over stocking stitch using 2¾ mm (UK 12/US 2) needles.

△ Rabbit finger puppet

RABBIT
BODY AND HEAD
With 2¾ mm (UK 12/US 2) needles and E, cast on 20 sts.
Knit 2 rows.
1st row: Knit.
2nd row: Purl.
Cont in st st until 12 rows have been worked.
Shape head
13th row: [K2tog, k1] 6 times, k2tog. (13 sts.)
14th row: Purl.
15th row: K1, inc 1 st in every st to end. (25 sts.)
Work in st st for 9 rows.

25th row: [K1, k2tog] 8 times, k1. (17 sts.)
26th row: Purl.
27th row: [K2tog, k1] 5 times, k2tog. (11 sts.)
Next row: [P2tog, p1] 3 times, p2tog. (7 sts.)
Break yarn, thread through rem sts, pull up tightly and fasten off securely. Sew seam.**

OUTER EARS [make 2]
With 2¾ mm (UK 12/US 2) needles and E, cast on 6 sts.
Work in g st for 10 rows.
11th row: K2tog, k2, k2tog. (4 sts.)
Cont in g st for 3 rows.

15th row: [K2tog] twice. (2 sts.)
16th row: K2tog. Fasten off.

INNER EARS [make 2]

With 2¾ mm (UK 12/US 2) needles and D, cast on
5 sts.
Work in st st for 10 rows.
11th row: Sl 1, k1, psso, k1, k2tog.
Work 3 rows.
15th row: Sl 1, k2tog, psso. Fasten off.
With WS of inner ear to outer ear, sew inner ear in
place. Make tuck in cast-on edge and sew cast-on
edges to head.

PAWS [make 2]

With 2¾ mm (UK 12/US 2) double-pointed needles
and E, cast on 8 sts.
1st row: K8, *do not turn, slide sts to opposite end of
needle and take yarn tightly across back of work,
knit 8 sts again, rep from * 4 times more, change to
A, work 2 more rows, do not turn, slide sts to
opposite end of needle and take yarn tightly across
back of work, [k2tog] 4 times, do not turn, slide sts to
opposite end of needle and take yarn tightly across
back of work, sl 1, k3tog, psso and fasten off. Insert
small amount of toy stuffing into paw, and then sew
cast-on end to body.

TO MAKE UP

Make small pompon using A and sew to back for tail.
Using Black, embroider French knots for eyes and
straight stitches for nose and mouth.

COW
BODY AND HEAD

Using A, work as for Body and Head of Rabbit.
Break yarn, thread through rem sts, pull up tightly
and fasten off securely. Sew seam.

EARS [make 1 in A, 1 in B]

With 2¾ mm (UK 12/US 2) needles, cast on 5 sts.
Work in g st for 8 rows.
5th row: K2tog, k1, k2tog. (3 sts.)
6th row: K3.
7th row: Sl 1, k2tog, psso. (1 st.)
Fasten off.
Fold sides of each ear at cast-on edges and attach to
head.

HORNS [make 2]

With 2¾ mm (UK 12/US 2) needles and C, cast on

△ *Cow finger puppet*

3 sts. Work in st st for 3 rows.
Next row: K3tog.
Fasten off. Attach horns to top of head between ears.

LEGS [make 2]

With 2¾ mm (UK 12/US 2) double-pointed needles
and A, cast on 8 sts.
1st row: K8, *do not turn, slide sts to opposite end of
needle and take yarn tightly across back of work, knit
8 sts again, rep from * 4 times more, change to C,
work 2 more rows, do not turn, slide sts to opposite
end of needle and take yarn tightly across back of
work, [k2tog] 4 times, do not turn, slide sts to
opposite end of needle and take yarn tightly across
back of work, sl 1, k3tog, psso and fasten off. Insert
small amount of toy stuffing into paw, and then sew
cast-on end to body. Make second leg, using B in
place of A.

TAIL

With A, make a twisted cord, approx 2 cm (¾ in) long.
With B, make a tassle, and attach to one end of tail.
Sew other end of tail to body.

MUZZLE

With 2¾ mm (UK 12/US 2) needles and C, cast on
3 sts.
Beg with a p row, work in st st at the same time inc

1 st at each end of next row. (5 sts.)
Next row: Inc 1 st, knit to last st, inc 1 st. (7 sts.)
Work 2 rows.
Next row: Dec 1 st, p to last st, dec 1 st. (5 sts.)
Next row: Dec 1 st, k to last st, dec 1 st. (3 sts.)
Cast off.

PATCH [make 1]

With 2¾ mm (UK 12/US 2) needles and B, cast on
3 sts.
Beg with a K row, work in st st, inc 1 st at each end of
next and foll alt row. (7 sts.)
Work 2 rows straight. Dec 1 st at each end of next
and foll alt row. (3 sts.) Cast off.

TO MAKE UP

Sew on muzzle. Using Black, embroider French knots
for eyes and nostrils, and stem stitch for mouth.

PIG

BODY AND HEAD

With 2¾ mm (UK 12/US 2) needles and D, cast on
20 sts.
Knit 2 rows.
**1st row: Knit.
2nd row: Purl.
Cont in st st until 12 rows have been worked.
Shape head
13th row: [K2tog, k1] 6 times, k2tog. (13 sts.)
14th row: Purl.
15th row: K1, inc 1 st in every st to end. (25 sts.)
Work in st st for 9 rows.
25th row: [K1, k2tog] 8 times, k1. (17 sts.)
26th row: Purl.
27th row: [K2tog, k1] 5 times, k2tog. (11 sts.)
Next row: [P2tog, p1] 3 times, p2tog. (7 sts.)
Break yarn, thread through rem sts, pull up tightly
and fasten off securely. Sew seam.**

EARS [make 2]

With 2¾ mm (UK 12/US 2) needles and D, cast on
5 sts.
Work in g st for 4 rows.
5th row: K2tog, k1, k2tog. (3 sts.)
6th row: K3.
7th row: Sl 1, k2tog, psso. (1 st.)
Fasten off. Sew cast-on edges of ears to sides of
head, gathering base slightly.

PAWS [make 2]

With 2¾ mm (UK 12/US 2) double-pointed needles

and D, cast on 8 sts.
1st row: K8, *do not turn, slide sts to opposite end of
needle and take yarn tightly across back of work, knit
8 sts again, rep from * 4 times more, change to C,
work 2 more rows, do not turn, slide sts to opposite
end of needle and take yarn tightly across back of
work, [k2tog] 4 times, do not turn, slide sts to
opposite end of needle and take yarn tightly across
back of work.
Sl 1, k3tog, psso and fasten off. Insert small amount
of toy stuffing into paw, and then sew cast-on end to
body.

SNOUT [make 1]

With 2¾ mm (UK 12/US 2) needles and C, cast on
4 sts.
Beg with a p row, work 7 rows in st st, inc 1 st at each
end of 2nd and foll alt row. (8 sts.)
8th row: K2tog, k4, k2tog. (6 sts.)
9th row: P6.
10th row: K2tog, k2, k2tog. (4 sts.)
Cast off rem 4 sts. Run gathering thread around outer
edge and pull up to form a snout.
Sew snout to front of head.

TAIL

With 2¾ mm (UK 12/US 2) needles and D, cast on
7 sts.
Work 2 rows knit. Cast off.

TO MAKE UP

Sew on snout.
Embroider French knots for eyes
using Black, and
nostrils using Dark
Pink. Embroider
mouth using stem
stitch.
Stuff head lightly,
stitch below head
shaping and fasten to
enclose stuffing.

▷ *Pig finger puppet*

MOUSE

BODY AND HEAD

Work in st st stripes as follows:

Work 2 rows B, 2 rows A.

Work as for Body and Head of Pig, working Head using A only.

OUTER EARS [make 2]

With 2¾ mm (UK 12/US 2) needles and A, cast on 5 sts.

Work in g st for 4 rows.

5th row: K2tog, k1, k2tog. (3 sts.)

6th row: Knit.

7th row: Sl 1, k2tog, psso. Fasten off.

INNER EARS [make 2]

With B, work as Outer Ears. Sew ears together, leaving cast-on edge open. Turn RS out, make tuck in cast-on edge and sew to head.

PAWS [make 2]

With 2¾ mm (UK 12/US 2) needles and B, work as for Paws of Bunny [working stripe pattern as set]. Insert small amount of toy stuffing into paw, and then sew cast-on end to body.

▽ *Mouse finger puppet*

TAIL

With 2¾ mm (UK 12/US 2) double-pointed needles and B, cast on 4 sts.

1st row: K4, *do not turn, slide sts to opposite end of needle and take yarn tightly across back of work, knit 4 sts again, rep from * for 8 cm, do not turn, slide sts to opposite end of needle and take yarn tightly across back of work, (k2tog) twice, do not turn, slide stitches to opposite end of needle and take yarn across back, k2tog, fasten off. Sew in place.

TO MAKE UP

Using Black, embroider French knots for eyes, satin stitch for nose and straight stitches for mouth.

△ *Lamb finger puppet*

LAMB

BODY AND HEAD

With 2¾ mm (UK 12/US 2) needles and F, cast on 20 sts.

Cont in g st until 16 rows have been worked.

Shape head

13th row: [K2tog, k1] 6 times, k2tog. (13 sts.)
14th row: Knit.
15th row: K1, inc 1 st in every st to end. (25 sts.)
16th row: K11F, p3A, k11F.
17th row: K11F, K3A, k11F.
18th row: K10F, p5A, k10F.
19th row: K10F, k5A, k10F.
Rep last 2 rows once more, then 18th row again.
23rd row: With F, knit.
24th row: With F, knit.
25th row: [K1, k2tog] 8 times. K1. (17 sts.)
26th row: Knit.
27th row: [K2tog, k1] 5 times, k2tog. (11 sts.)
Next row: [K2tog, k1] 3 times, k2tog. (7 sts.)
Break yarn, thread through rem sts, pull up tightly and fasten off securely. Sew seam.

EARS (make 2)

With 2¾ mm (UK 12/US 2) needles and C, cast on 7 sts.

Work in g st for 6 rows.
7th row: K2tog, k3, k2tog. (5 sts.)
8th row: K2tog, k1, k2tog. (3 sts.)
Cast off rem sts.
Sew cast-on edges of ears to sides of head, gathering base slightly.

LEGS (make 2)

With 2¾ mm (UK 12/US 2) double-pointed needles and F, cast on 8 sts.

1st row: Moss st 8 sts, *do not turn, slide sts to opposite end of needle and take yarn tightly across back of work, moss st 8 sts again, rep from * 4 times more, change to C, work 2 rows in st st, cont in st st, do not turn, slide sts to opposite end of needle and take yarn tightly across back of work, [k2tog] 4 times, do not turn, slide sts to opposite end of needle and take yarn tightly across back of work, sl 1, k3tog, psso and fasten off.

Insert small amount of toy stuffing into paw, and then sew cast-on end to body.

TO MAKE UP

Using E, embroider French knots for eyes, satin stitch for nose and straight stitches for mouth.

Tropical fish

With its vibrant blocks of colour and big kissing lips, who could resist this delightful tropical fish. If you really like them, why not make a whole aquarium of fish in brilliant colours – just choose your favourite shades and tones in Handknit DK Cotton.

MEASUREMENTS
24 cm (9½ in) long

MATERIALS
• Oddments of Rowan Handknit DK Cotton in Orange (MC), Yellow (A), Blue (B), Green (C) and Red (D)
• Washable toy stuffing
• Pair of 3¼ mm (UK 10/US 3) knitting needles

ABBREVIATIONS
See page 14.

TENSION
24 sts and 32 rows to 10 cm (4 in) measured over stocking stitch using 3¼ mm (UK 10/US 3) needles.

BODY
With 3¼ mm (UK 10/US 3) needles and MC, cast on 8 sts.
Work in st st throughout.
1st row: Knit.
2nd row: Purl.
3rd row: Cast on 2 sts, k to end.
4th row: Cast on 3 sts, p to end.
Rep last 2 rows twice more.
9th row: As 3rd row. (25 sts.)
10th row: Inc 1 st, p to last st, inc in last st. (27 sts.)
11th row: Inc 1 st, k to last st, inc in last st. (29 sts.)
12th row: Inc 1 st, p to last st, inc in last st with A. (31 sts.)
13th row: With A, inc 1 st, k2 A, with MC k to last st, inc in last st. (33 sts.)

14th row: With MC, inc 1 st, p to last 5 sts, with A, p to last st, inc in last st. (35 sts.)
15th row: With A, inc 1 st, k6 A, with MC k to last st, inc in last st. (37 sts.)
16th row: With MC, p to last 8 sts, with A, p to end. (37 sts.)
17th row: With A, inc 1 st, k8 A, with MC, k to end, inc in last st. (39 sts.)
18th row: With MC, p to last 10 sts, with A, p to end.
19th row: With A, inc 1 st, k10 A, with MC, k to last st, inc in last st. (41 sts.)
20th row: With MC, inc 1 st, p to last 12 sts, with A, p to last st, inc in last st. (43 sts.)
21st row: K13 A, with MC, k to end.
22nd row: With MC, p to last 13 sts, with A, p to end.
23rd row: As 21st row.
24th row: With MC, p2tog, p to last 12 sts, with A, p10, p2tog. (41 sts.)
25th row: With A, k2tog, k10 A, with MC, k to last 2 sts, k2tog. (39 sts.)
26th row: With MC, p to last 9 sts, with A, p7, p2tog, dec in last st. (38 sts.)
27th row: With A, k2tog, k6 A, with MC, k to last 2 sts, k2tog. (36 sts.)
28th row: With MC, p to last 6 sts, with A, p to end.
29th row: With A, k2tog, k4 A, with MC, k to last 2 sts, k2tog. (34 sts.)
30th row: With MC, p2tog, p to last 4 sts, with A, p2, p2tog. (32 sts.)
31st row: With A, k2tog, with MC, k to last 2 sts, k2tog. (30 sts.)
32nd row: With MC, p2tog, p to last 2 sts, k2tog. (28 sts.)
33rd row: With MC, k2tog, k to last 2 sts, k2tog. (26 sts.)

34th row: With MC, p2tog, p to last p to last 2 sts, p2tog. (24 sts.)
35th row: With MC, cast off 2, k to end.
36th row: With MC, cast off 3, p to end.
37th row: With MC, cast off 2, k to end.
Rep last 2 rows twice more.
Work 1 row. Cast off 7 rem sts.

TAIL [make 2]
With 3¼ mm (UK 10/US 3) needles and C, cast on 8 sts.
Work 4 rows in st st.
5th row: Inc 1 st at each end of row. (10 sts.)
6th row: Purl.
Rep last rows twice more. (14 sts.)
11th row: Inc 1 st, k6, turn, leave rem sts on a spare needle.
12th row: P8.
13th row: K8.
Rep last 2 rows once more.
16th row: P2tog, p to end.
17th row: K to last 2 sts, k2tog.
Rep last 2 rows twice more.
22nd row: P2tog, fasten off.
Rejoin yarn to rem sts, k to last st, inc 1 st. (8 sts.)
Next row: P8.

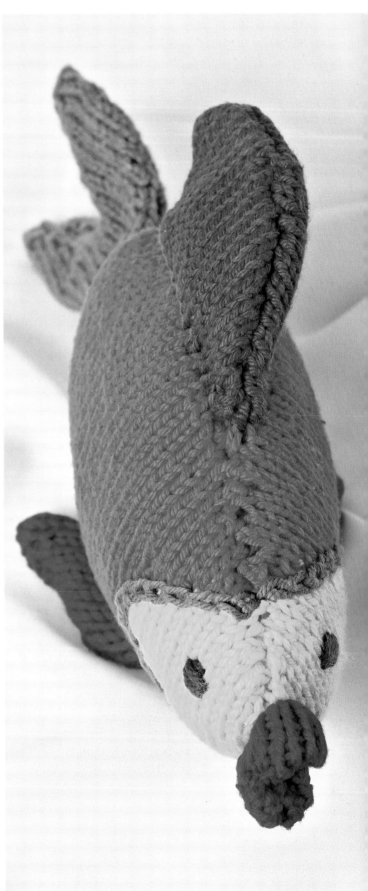

Next row: K8.
Rep last 2 rows once more.
Next row: P to last 2 sts, p2tog.
Next row: K2tog, k to end.
Rep last 2 rows twice more.
22nd row: P2tog, fasten off.

TOP FIN [A]

With 3¼ mm (UK 10/US 3) needles and B, cast on
17 sts.
1st row: Knit.
2nd row: Purl.
3rd row: Inc 1 st, k to end.
4th row: Dec 1 st, p to end.
Rep last rows twice more. (17 sts.)
9th row: Knit.
10th row: Dec 1 st, p to end. (16 sts.)
11th row: Knit.
12th row: Cast off 3, p to end. (13 sts.)
13th row: Inc 1 st, k to end. (14 sts.)
14th row: Cast off 5, p to end. (9 sts.)
15th row: Knit.
Cast off rem 9 sts.

TOP FIN [B]

With 3¼ mm (UK 10/US 3) needles and B, cast on
17 sts.
1st row: Purl.
2nd row: Knit.
Work fin as set for Top Fin A, reversing all shapings.

LOWER FIN [C] [make 2]

With 3¼ mm (UK 10/US 3) needles and D, cast on
8 sts.
1st row: Knit.
2nd row: Purl.
3rd row: Knit.
4th row: Inc 1 st, p to end. (9 sts.)
5th row: Knit.
6th row: Inc 1 st, p to end. (10 sts.)
7th row: K2tog, k to end. (9 sts.)
8th row: Purl.
9th row: Dec 1 st, k to last st, inc 1 st. (9 sts.)
10th row: P to last 2 sts, p2tog.
11th row: Dec 1 st, k to end.
Rep last 2 rows once more. (5 sts.)
14th row: As 10th row.
Cast off rem 4 sts.

LOWER FIN [D] [make 2]

With 3¼ mm (UK 10/US 3) needles and D, cast on
8 sts.
Work fin as set for Lower Fin C, reversing all
shapings.

LIPS [make 2]

With 3¼ mm (UK 10/US 3) needles and D, cast on
8 sts.
1st row: Knit.
2nd row: Purl.
3rd row: Cast on 2, k to end.
4th row: Cast on 3, p to end. (11 sts.)
Rep last 2 rows twice more. (21 sts.)
Inc 1 st at each end of next 4 rows. (29 sts.)
Cast off.

TO MAKE UP

Using C, embroider chain stitch line across body
sections where MC and A meet.
Join body seam neatly, leaving a small opening, stuff
then stitch up small opening.
Sew tail together, sew cast-on edge to end of body.
Stitch top fins A and B together.
Sew cast-on edges to top edge of body.
Stitch lower fins C and D together.
Sew cast-on edges to lower edge of body.
Using B, embroider spot for eye in satin stitch.
Oversew lip rows together tightly, form a "heart"
shape, then sew mouth on to front of body as shown
on photograph.

Caterpillar finger puppets

These brightly coloured finger puppets will give children hours of enjoyment and are ideal for young children having fun with their own puppet shows.

MEASUREMENTS
8 cm (3 in) tall

MATERIALS
• Oddments of Patons Diploma Gold DK in Pink (A), Apple Green (B), Yellow (C), Aqua (D), Violet (E), Orange (F) and Black (for embroidery)
• Small amount washable toy stuffing
• Pair 3 mm (UK 11/US 2/3) knitting needles

ABBREVIATIONS
See page 14.

TENSION
28 sts and 38 rows to 10 cm (4 in) measured over stocking stitch using 3 mm (UK 11/US 2/3) needles.

▽ Caterpillar 1

CATERPILLAR 1
BODY AND HEAD
With 3 mm (UK 11/US 2/3) needles and A, cast on 20 sts.
Knit 2 rows.
Now work in st st stripes as follows: 2 rows A, 2 rows B.
Cont in stripes until 12 rows have been worked.
Shape head
*13th row: With B only, (k2tog, k1) 6 times, k2tog. (13 sts.)
14th row: Purl.
15th row: Inc in each st to last st, k1. (25 sts.)
Work in st st for 9 rows.
25th row: [K1, k2tog] 8 times, k1. (17 sts.)
26th row: Purl.
27th row: [K2tog, k1] 5 times, k2tog. (11 sts.)

28th row: [P2tog, p1] 3 times, p2tog. (7 sts.)
Break yarn, thread through rem sts, pull up tightly and fasten off securely. *

ANTENNAE [make 2]
Using C, work as follows:
**With 3 mm (UK 11/US 2/3) needles, cast on 1 st.
Make bobble as follows:
[K1, p1, k1] all into next st, turn, k3, turn, and p3, turn and sl 1, k2tog, psso. Pull up and fasten off, making into a bobble.
Make antenna
Cast on 4 sts, work 4 rows st st. Cast off.
Roll along from cast-on edge to cast-off edge and stitch along edge neatly.
Sew bobble into place to row side (top of antenna).**

RIGHT LEGS [make 3]

Using B, work as follows:

*** With 3 mm (UK 11/US 2/3) needles, cast on 4 sts, and work in g st for 2 rows.

Cast off 2 sts, work on rem 2 sts.

K into front and back of next 2 sts. (4 sts.)

Next row: P4.

Next row: K4.

Rep last 2 rows twice more.

Next row: K4.

Cast off rem 4 sts.

Sew seam edges neatly.***

LEFT LEGS [make 3]

Using B, work as follows:

**** With 3 mm (UK 11/US 2/3) needles, cast on 4 sts, and work in g st for 2 rows.

Cast off 2 sts, work on rem 2 sts.

P into front and back of next 2 sts. (4 sts.)

Next row: K4.

Next row: P4.

Rep last 2 rows twice more.

Next row: K4.

Cast off rem 4 sts.

Sew seam edges neatly.****

TO MAKE UP

Join seam neatly on body.

Stuff head lightly, stitch below head shaping and fasten to enclose stuffing.

Sew antennae to top of head.

Sew legs on to body.

Using Black, embroider French knots for eyes and stem stitch for mouth

Using pink, work in satin st to embroider nose.

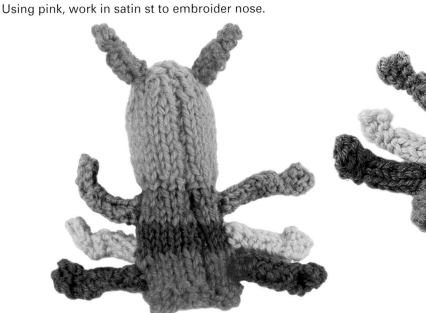

CATERPILLAR 2

BODY AND HEAD

With 3 mm (UK 11/US 2/3) needles and F, cast on 20 sts.

Knit 2 rows.

Now work in st st stripes as follows: 4 rows F, 4 rows E, 4 rows D. (12 rows.)

Shape head

With A only, work as Caterpillar 1, from * to *.

ANTENNAE [make 2] in F

Work as Caterpillar 1, from ** to **.

RIGHT LEGS [make 3] 1 in B, 1 in C, 1 in E

Work as Caterpillar 1, from *** to ***.

LEFT LEGS [make 3] 1 in B, 1 in C, 1 in E

Work as Caterpillar 1, from **** to ****.

TO MAKE UP

Join seam neatly on body.

Stuff head lightly, stitch below head shaping and fasten to enclose stuffing.

Sew antennae to top of head.

Sew legs on to body.

Using Black, embroider French knots for eyes and stem stitch for mouth.

Using E, embroider nose in satin stitch.

▽ *Caterpillar 2*

▷ Caterpillar 3

CATERPILLAR 3

BODY AND HEAD

With 3 mm (UK 11/US 2/3) needles and C, cast on 16 sts.

Knit 2 rows.

Now work in st st stripes as follows: 2 rows C, 2 rows F, 2 rows B, 2 rows E, 2 rows A, 2 rows D. (12 rows.)

Work shaping as follows:

Next row: With C, k1, * ml, k4; rep from * to last 3 sts, m1, k3. (20 sts.)

Next row: With C, purl.

Next row: With F, k1, * m1, k5; rep from * to last 4 sts, m1, k4. (24 sts.)

Next row: With F, purl.

Next row: With B, k1, *m1, k6; rep from * to last 5 sts, m1, k5. (28 sts.)

Next row: With B, purl.

Next row: With E, knit.

Next row: With E, purl.

Next row: With A, k1, * k2tog, k5; rep from * to last 6 sts, k2tog, k4. (24 sts.)

Next row: With A, purl.

Next row: With D, k1, * k2tog, k4; rep from * to last 5 sts, k2tog, k3. (20 sts.)

Next row: With D, purl.

Next row: With C, knit.

Next row: With C, purl.

Shape head

With F only, work as Caterpillar 1, from * to *.

ANTENNAE [make 2] in A

Work as Caterpillar 1, from ** to **.

RIGHT LEGS [make 3] in C

Work as Caterpillar 1, from *** to ***.

LEFT LEGS [make 3] in C

Work as Caterpillar 1, from **** to ****.

HAT

***** With 3 mm (UK 11/US 2/3) needles and E, cast on 25 sts.

Work in st st for 12 rows.

Shape top

13th row: [K1, k2tog] 8 times, k1. (18 sts.)

14th row: Purl.

15th row: [K2tog, k1] 6 times. (12 sts.)

Next row: [P2tog, p1] 4 times. (8 sts.)

Break yarn, thread through rem sts, pull up tightly and fasten off securely. Sew seam, reversing seam on first 4 rows.*****

TO MAKE UP

Join seam neatly on body. Stuff head lightly, stitch below head shaping and fasten to enclose stuffing.

Sew antennae to hat.

Sew legs on to body.

Using Black, embroider French knots for eyes and stem stitch for mouth. Using A, embroider nose in satin stitch.

CATERPILLAR 4
BODY AND HEAD
With 3 mm (UK 11/US 2/3) needles and C, cast on 20 sts.

1st row: [WS] Knit.
2nd row: [RS] Purl.
Rep last 2 rows twice.
7th row: Purl.
Change to B, k 1 row.
Work from 1st to 7th row.
Change to E, k 1 row.
Work from 1st to 7th row. (24 rows.)
Shape head
With D only, work as Caterpillar 1, from * to *.

ANTENNAE [make 2] in B
Work as Caterpillar 1, from ** to **.

RIGHT LEGS [make 3] in A
Work as Caterpillar 1, from *** to ***.

LEFT LEGS [make 3] in A
Work as Caterpillar 1, from **** to ****.

TO MAKE UP
On WS of body, slip stitch the 8 rows together; this will form 3 ridges on RS.
Join seam neatly on body.
Stuff head lightly, stitch below head shaping and fasten to enclose stuffing.
Sew antennae to top of head.
Sew legs on to body.
Using Black, embroider French knots for eyes and stem stitch for mouth.
Using A, embroider nose in satin stitch.

CATERPILLAR 5
BODY AND HEAD
With 3 mm (UK 11/US 2/3) needles and F, cast on 20 sts.

1st row: [WS] With F, knit.
2nd row: [RS] With F, purl.
3rd row: With F, knit.
4th row: With C, knit.
5th row: With C, knit.
6th row: With C, purl.
7th row: With C, knit.
With D, work from rows 4 to 7.
With E, work from rows 4 to 7.
With B, work from rows 4 to 7. (19 rows.)
Shape head
With C only, work as Caterpillar 1, from * to *.

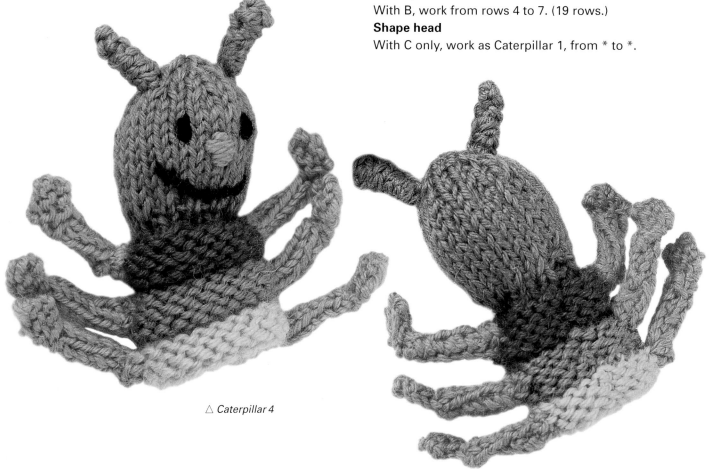

△ Caterpillar 4

ANTENNAE [make 2] in E
Work as Caterpillar 1, from ** to **.

RIGHT LEGS [make 3] 1 in A, 1 in C and 1 in E
Work as Caterpillar 1, from *** to ***.

LEFT LEGS [make 3] 1 in A, 1 in C and 1 in E
Work as Caterpillar 1, from **** to ****.

HAT in A
Work as Caterpillar 3, from ***** to *****.

TO MAKE UP
Join seam neatly on body.
Stuff head lightly, stitch below head shaping and fasten to enclose stuffing.
Sew antennae to top of hat.
Sew legs on to body.
Using Black, embroider French knots for eyes and stem stitch for mouth.
Using A, embroider nose in satin stitch.

▽ *Caterpillar 5*

Fairy

This pretty little fairy with her delicate wings and golden hair is a lovely toy for a little girl's bedroom. She would also be a perfect adornment for the top of a Christmas tree.

SKILL LEVEL 1

MEASUREMENTS
Approximately 26 cm (10 in) tall

MATERIALS
- 1 x 50 g ball of Rowan 4 ply Cotton in Pink (A)
- 1 x 50 g ball of Rowan Kidsilk Haze in White (B)
- 1 x 50 g ball of Rowan Lurex Shimmer in Pewter (C)
- Oddments of yellow, black and pink 4 ply wool
- Washable toy stuffing
- Pair each of 2¾ mm (UK 12/US 2) and 3 mm (UK 11/US 2/3) knitting needles
- 2.50 mm (UK 12/US C2) crochet hook

ABBREVIATIONS
See page 14.

TENSION
4 ply cotton tension:
32 sts and 42 rows to 10 cm (4 in) measured over stocking stitch using 2¾ mm (UK 12/US 2) needles.
Kidsilk Haze tension:
25 sts and 34 rows to 10 cm (4 in) measured over stocking stitch using 3 mm (UK 11/US 2/3) needles.

FAIRY
BODY
Back and front [alike]
With 2¾ mm (UK 12/US 2) needles and A, cast on 20 sts.
Work in st st for 24 rows, ending with a WS row.
Shape body
Dec 1 st at each end on every row 4 times. (12 sts.)
Dec 1 st at each end of every alt row until 6 sts rem.
Work 1 row.
Shape head
Inc 1 st at each end on every row 3 times. (12 sts.)
Inc 1 st at each end on next 2 alt rows. (16 sts.)
Work 9 rows straight.
Dec 1 st at each end on next row. (14 sts.)
Work 1 row straight.
Dec 1 st at each end on next 2 rows. (10 sts.)
Cast off 2 sts at beg of next 2 rows. (6 sts.)
Cast off rem 6 sts.

LEGS AND ARMS [make 4]
With A, make twisted cord using 4 strands of yarn.
[Finished length 10 cm/4 in].

SHOES [make 2]
With 3 mm (UK 11/US 2/3) needles and C, cast on
16 sts.
Work in g st as follows:
Dec 1 st at each end of every alt row until 8 sts rem.
Work 2 rows. Cast off.
Fold in half, sew round edges.

HANDS [make 2]
With 2¾ mm (UK 12/US 2) needles and A, cast on
2 sts.
Work in g st as follows:
 Inc 1 st at each end of every alt row until there are
   6 sts.
     Work straight for 2 rows.
       Dec 1 st at each end of every alt row until there
       are 4 sts. Cast off.

DRESS [back and front alike]
 With 3 mm (UK 11/US 2/3) needles and B, cast on
40 sts.
Work in st st throughout, at the same time dec
1 st at each end of 3rd and foll 2 alt rows. (34 sts.)
Now dec 1 st at each end of every 5th row, 5 times.
(24 sts.)
Now dec 1 st at each end of every 4th row, 4 times.
(16 sts.)
 Next row: Knit.
  Next row: [P2tog] 8 times. (8 sts.)
Cast off rem sts.

SLEEVES [make 2]
With 3 mm (UK 11/US 2/3) needles and B, cast on
10 sts.
Work in st st throughout, at the same time dec 1 st at
each end of every 4th row, 3 times. Work 4 rows
straight. (4 sts.) K2tog twice. (2 sts.)
Cast off.

WINGS
With 3 mm (UK 11/US 2/3) needles and B, cast on
8 sts.
Work in g st throughout, at the same time cast on
4 sts at beg of next 8 rows. (40 sts.)
Work 2 rows straight.
Cast off 2 sts at beg of next 4 rows. (32 sts.)
K 16 sts, turn, leave rem sts on a spare needle.

Cast off 2 sts at beg of next 8 rows. Fasten off.
Rejoin yarn to 16 sts, cast off 2 sts at beg of next
8 rows. Fasten off.

TO MAKE UP BODY
Place RS of front and back of body together.
Sew edges together, leaving small gap at bottom of
body.
Turn the body RS out. Stuff, then sew up small gap.
Attach legs to bottom of body, with a space of 2 cm
(¾ in) apart. Sew on shoes.
Attach arms to upper part of body into side seams,
1 cm (¼ in) down from neck. Sew on hands.
Embroider French knots for eyes and satin stitch for
nose using Black. Embroider stem stitch for mouth
using Pink.

HAIR
Cut 30 lengths of yellow yarn approx 25½ cm (10 in)
long. Using backstitch, stitch to centre of head to
form hair. Strand yarn carefully to form "curly" hair.
With C, tie "hair" into pig tails.

TO MAKE UP
Join raglan seams of dress to sleeves.
Join side and sleeve seams.
Put dress on to doll.

HEM EDGING
With 2.50 mm (UK 12/US C2) crochet hook and C,
work a row of dc along cast-on edge of dress, then
work as follows:
1 dc into the first st, *3ch, miss one st, 1 dc into next
st, rep from * to end. Fasten off.

NECK EDGING
Work as hem edging.

CUFF EDGING
Work as hem edging.

WING EDGING
Work as hem edging. Sew wings on to back of dress.

Turtle

This colourful turtle makes a lovely soft toy with its large "cushioned" shell. The turtle's hat is decorated with a lazy daisy stitch.

SKILL LEVEL 2

MEASUREMENTS
23 cm (9 in) long

MATERIALS
• 1 x 50 g ball of Patons Diploma Gold DK in Green
• Small amounts of Red, Yellow, Orange, Violet, Bright Aqua and Blue
• Washable toy stuffing
• Pair of 3 mm (UK 11/US 2/3) knitting needles

ABBREVIATIONS
See page 14.

TENSION
24 sts and 32 rows to 10 cm (4 in) measured over stocking stitch using 3 mm (UK 11/US 2/3) needles.

NOTE: Moss stitch used for turtle shell throughout.

CENTRE SHELL
With 3 mm (UK 11/US 2/3) needles and Green, cast on 3 sts.
1st row: K1, p1, k1.
Cont in moss st, inc 1 st at each end of next and foll 2 alt rows. (9 sts.)
Work 3 rows in moss st.
Dec 1 st at each end of next and foll 2 alt rows. (3 sts.)
Work 1 row.
Cast off.

SHELL SIDES (make 1 red, yellow, orange, violet, blue)
With 3 mm (UK 11/US 2/3) needles, cast on 3 sts.
1st row: K1, p1, k1.
Cont in moss st, inc 1 st at each end of next and foll 5 alt rows. (15 sts.)
Work 3 rows in moss st.

Cont in moss st, dec 1 st at each end of next and foll 3 alt rows. (7 sts.)
Work 1 row.
Cast off.

SHELL EDGINGS (make 5 Green)
With 3 mm (UK 11/US 2/3) needles, cast on 3 sts.
1st row: K1, p1, k1.
Cont in moss st, inc 1 st at each end of next and foll 7 alt rows. (19 sts.)
Work in moss st for 2 rows.
Cast off.

UNDERBODY (make 1)
With 3 mm (UK 11/US 2/3) needles and Green, cast on 11 sts.
Work in moss st for 1 row. Inc at each end of next row and foll 8 alt rows. (29 sts.)

Cont in moss st for 28 rows.
Dec 1 st at each end of next and foll 8 alt rows.
(11 sts.)
Work in moss st for 1 row. Cast off.

FEET (make 4)

With 3 mm (UK 11/US 2/3) needles and Green, cast on 18 sts.
Work 14 rows in st st. Cast off.

HEAD

With 3 mm (UK 11/US 2/3) needles and Green, cast on 20 sts.
Work 2 rows in st st.
Next row: Inc in first st, k8, inc in each of next 2 sts, k8, inc in last st. (24 sts.)
P 1 row.
Next row: Inc in first st, k10, inc in each of next 2 sts, k10, inc in last st. (28 sts.)
Work in st st for 4 rows.
Next row: K1, *k2tog, k2; rep from * to last 3 sts, k2tog, k1. (21 sts.)
Work in st st for 2 rows.
Cast off.

TAIL

With 3 mm (UK 11/US 2/3) needles and Green, cast on 10 sts.
Work 8 rows in st st.
Next row: [K2tog] 5 times. (5 sts.)
Break yarn, thread through rem sts, pull up tightly and fasten off securely.

HAT

With 3 mm (UK 11/US 2/3) needles and Blue, cast on 13 sts, work in moss st for 6 rows.
Next row: K1, (k2tog) 6 times. (7 sts.)
Break yarn, thread rem sts, pull up and fasten off securely. Join side seam.

BRIM

With 3 mm (UK 11/US 2/3) needles and Red, cast on 30 sts.
Work in st st for 4 rows. Cast off.

TO MAKE UP

Join shells together, green to be in centre, blue to be attached to red, red to violet, violet to orange, orange to yellow. Sew shell edgings to sides of shells to complete upper section.
Stitch top to base, leaving a small gap for stuffing. Insert stuffing and close opening.
Join side and cast-on edges of legs, head and tail. Fill with stuffing and attach close to edge of shell.
Sew hat to head, inserting stuffing. Join ends of brim, then sew cast-on edge of brim to point where hat joins to head.
With Blue, embroider eyes using French knots.
With Red, embroider the mouth using stem stitch.
With Yellow, embroider flower on hat using lazy daisy stitch (see page 12). With Blue, embroider centre of flower using a French knot.

Princess

This pretty princess is knitted in luxury 4 ply cotton, Kidsilk and Lurex shimmer in beautiful purples and pinks. Make your own little princess feel special with this charming toy.

SKILL LEVEL 2

MEASUREMENTS
Approximately 33 cm (13 in) tall

MATERIALS
- 2 x 50 g balls of Rowan 4 ply Cotton in Pink (MC)
- 2 x 50 g balls of Rowan 4 ply Cotton in Mauve (B)
- Small amount of Rowan 4 ply Cotton in White (A)
- Small amount of Rowan Lurex Shimmer in Mauve (C)
- Small amount of Rowan Kidsilk Haze in Mauve (D)
- Oddments of Yellow, Black and Pink 4 ply wool
- Washable toy stuffing
- Pair each of 2¾ mm (UK 12/US 2) and 3 mm (UK 11/US 2/3) knitting needles
- 2.50 mm (UK 12/US C2) crochet hook

ABBREVIATIONS
See page 14.

TENSION
4 ply cotton tension for body:
32 sts and 42 rows to 10 cm (4 in) measured over stocking stitch using 2¾ mm (UK 12/US 2) needles.
4 ply cotton tension for dress:
29 sts and 39 rows to 10 cm (4 in) measured over stocking stitch using 3 mm (UK 11/US 2/3) needles.
Kidsilk Haze tension for sleeves:
25 sts and 34 rows to 10 cm (4 in) measured over stocking stitch using 3 mm (UK 11/US 2/3) needles.

PRINCESS
1ST LEG
With 2¾ mm (UK 12/US 2) needles and MC, cast on 18 sts.
Work 12 rows in st st.
Shape heel: K 9 sts, turn, sl 1, p7, turn, sl 1, k6, turn. Continue until p 3, then turn. Sl 1, k2, turn, sl 1, p to end.
Work straight in st st for 44 rows. Cast off.
2ND LEG
Work as first leg, working heel on last 9 sts on needle instead of first 9 sts.

BODY
With 2¾ mm (UK 12/US 2) needles and A, cast on 44 sts.
Work in st st as follows:
Work 2 row A, 2 rows MC for 10 rows.
Using MC throughout.
Work 24 rows, ending with a WS row.
Shape armholes: K10 sts, cast off 2, k to last 12 sts, cast off 2, k to end.
Work on these last 10 sts in st st.
Work 1 row.
Next row: RS facing: Dec 1, k to end. (9 sts.)
Work straight in st st for 5 rows.
Next row: Cast off 5 sts, k4. Break yarn.

FRONT
Rejoin yarn to centre 20 sts with WS facing.
Work 1 row.
Dec 1 st at each end of next row. (18 sts.)
Work straight for 5 rows.
Next row: Cast off 5 sts, k to last 5 sts, cast off rem 5 sts. Break yarn.

LEFT BACK
Rejoin yarn to rem 10 sts with WS facing and work 1 row.
Dec 1 st at end of next row.

Work straight for 5 rows.
Next row: K4, cast off 5 sts. Break yarn.
With RS facing k across all neck sts, inc 4 sts evenly.
(20 sts.)
Work 3 rows st st.

HEAD

Knit into front and back of every st. (40 sts.)
Cast on 1 st at beg of next 4 rows. (44 sts.)
Work 13 rows straight.
Next row: *K2tog, k9; rep from * to end. (40 sts.)
Next row: Purl.
Next row: *K2tog, k8; rep from * to end. (36 sts.)
Dec as set until 20 sts rem.
Break off yarn and thread through rem sts.

ARMS (make 2)

With 2¾ mm (UK 12/US 2) needles and MC, cast on
4 sts.
Work 6 rows in st st.
Break yarn and set these thumb sts to one side.
With 2¾ mm (UK 12/US 2) needles and MC, cast on
12 sts.
Work 8 rows in st st. Break yarn.
Next row: K4 thumb sts, then k12 from "hand".
Work 5 rows st st.
7th row: K2tog, k14. (15 sts.)
Work 32 rows straight.
Dec 1 st at beg of next row and at same edge on foll
3 rows. (11 sts.)
Work 4 rows straight.
Dec 1 st at beg of next row and at same edge on foll
3 rows. (7 sts.)
Cast off.

TO MAKE UP

Join leg seams and stuff. Join arm seams and stuff.
Attach legs to cast-on edge of body, leaving a small
gap for crotch. Sew up back seam.
Set arms into armholes. Stuff body and head.
Using Black, embroider French knots for eyes and satin
stitch for nose. Embroider mouth using stem stitch and
Pink.
Cut lengths of yellow yarn approx 33 cm (13 in) long.
Using backstitch, stitch to centre of head to form hair.
Plait hair at side of face and secure. With C, make
tightly twisted strand of yarn to hold in place.

SOCKS
1ST SOCK
With 2¾ mm (UK 12/US 2) needles and A, cast on
18 sts.
Work 12 rows in st st.
Shape heel
K9 sts, turn, sl 1, p7, turn, sl 1, k6, turn.
Continue until p3, then turn. Sl 1, k2, turn, sl 1, p to end.
Work straight in st st for 10 rows. Cast off.
2ND SOCK
Work as first sock, working heel on last 9 sts on needle
instead of first 9 sts. Join seam.

EDGING ON SOCKS
With 2.50 mm (UK 12/US C2) crochet hook and A, work
a row of dc along top edge of socks, then work as
follows:
1 dc into the first st, *3 ch, miss one st, 1 dc into next
st, rep from * to end.
Fasten off.

SHOES (make 2)
With 2¾ mm (UK 12/US 2) needles and B, cast on
9 sts.
Work in st st, inc 1 st at beg of every row until there are
15 sts.
K2tog at beg of every row until 9 sts rem.
Cast on 6 sts, k to end. (15 sts.) Inc 1 st at beg of next
and every alt row until there are 18 sts.
Next row: [RS] Cast off 10 sts, k to end. (8 sts.)
Work 9 rows. Cast on 10 sts at beg of next row. (18 sts.)
Dec 1 st at beg of next and every alt row until 15 sts
rem.
Cast off.
Sew heel and sole seams.
Make ties:
Cut two 18-cm (7-in) lengths of C, thread through top of
shoes and tie in bow to form laces.

DRESS
FRONT
With 3 mm (UK 11/US 2/3) needles and B, cast on 72 sts.

Work in st st throughout until 40 rows have been worked.

Next row: [RS] k2, [k2tog] to last 2 sts, k2. (38 sts.)

Next row: P2, [p2tog] to last 2 sts, p2. (21 sts.)

Work 4 rows straight.

Shape armholes
Cast off 2 sts at beg of next 2 rows. (17 sts.)

Dec 1 st at each end of next row. (15 sts.)

Work straight for in st st for 11 rows.

Shape front neck
RS facing: K4, leave rem sts on a spare needle. Work a further 3 rows straight on these 4 sts. Cast off. Rejoin yarn to rem sts with RS facing, cast off centre 7 sts, k to end. Work a further 3 rows straight on these 4 sts. Cast off.

BACK
With 3 mm (UK 11/US 2/3) needles and B, cast on 72 sts.

Work in st st throughout until 40 rows have been worked.

Next row: [RS] k2, [k2tog], to last 2 sts, k2. (38 sts.)

Next row: P2, [p2tog] to last 2 sts, p2. (21 sts.)

Work 4 rows straight.

Shape armholes
Cast off 2 sts at beg of next 2 rows. (17 sts.)

Dec 1 st at each end of next row. (15 sts.)

Work 1 row.

Divide for back opening
K 7, leave rem sts on a spare needle. Work straight for a further 10 rows.

WS facing: Cast off 2 sts, p to end. (5 sts.) Dec 1 st at neck edge on next row. (4 sts.)

Work 1 row straight. Cast off rem sts.

Return to rem sts left on spare needle, k2tog, k to end. (7 sts.) Work 9 rows.

Cast off 2 sts at beg of next row. (5 sts.)

Dec 1 st at neck edge on next row. Work straight for 2 rows. Cast off rem sts.

SLEEVES
With 3 mm (UK 11/US 2/3) needles and D, cast on 25 sts, work in st st for 16 rows. Cast off.

With 2¾ mm (UK 12/US 2) needles and C, cast on 3 sts, work in g st until work measures 4.5 cm (1¾ in) (width of arm). Cast off.

PETALS [make 10]
With 3 mm (UK 11/US 2/3) needles and D, cast on 2 sts. Inc 1 st at each end of foll 3 rows. (8 sts.) Work straight for 9 rows.

Dec 1 st at each end of foll alt rows twice. Work 1 row. Cast off rem 4 sts.

TO MAKE UP
Join shoulder seams. Set in sleeves, gathering sleeves at top. Gather lower edge and sew g st band to cast-on edge of sleeves.

Join side and sleeve seams.

BODICE BAND
With 2¾ mm (UK 12/US 2) needles and C, cast on 3 sts, work in g st until work measures 26 cm (10 in). Cast off.

HEM EDGING
With a 2.50 mm (UK 12/US C2) crochet hook and C, work a row of dc along cast-on edge of dress, then work as follows:

1 dc into the first st, *3 ch, miss 1 st, 1 dc into next st, rep from * to end.

NECK EDGING
Work as hem edging.

Cut 25-cm (10-in) lengths of C and attach centre of each length to neck edge at top of back opening. Tie in bow to fasten neck.

Sew petals in place on Back and Front, gathering petals.

Sew bodice band in place neatly starting and finishing at centre back, just covering top of petals. Tie bow.

With C, embroider "stars" round lower edge of "skirt" part of dress (see page 12).

CROWN
With 2¾ mm (UK 12/US 2) needles and C, cast on 2 sts.

1st row: Knit.

2nd row: Knit.

3rd row: Cast on 2 sts, k to end.

4th row: Knit.

5th row: Cast off 2 sts, k to end.

Rep from 2nd to 5th row 15 times more, or until long enough to fit round head. Cast off.

Join cast-on and cast-off seams.

Monkey

This cheeky knitted toy is great for your own little monkeys and will appeal to anyone with a sense of fun. Rowan Kid Classic is a lovely soft yarn, making this a cuddly toy as well.

MEASUREMENTS
38 cm (15 in) tall

MATERIALS
- 1 x 50 g ball of Rowan Kid Classic in Medium Brown (MC)
- 1 x 50 g ball of Rowan Kid Classic in Light Brown (A)
- Small amount Black for embroidery
- Pair 3¾ mm (UK 9/US 5) knitting needles
- Washable toy stuffing

ABBREVIATIONS
See page 14.

TENSION
20 sts and 27 rows to 10 cm (4 in) measured over stocking stitch using 3¾ mm (UK 9/US 5) needles.

LEGS
With 3¾ mm (UK 9/US 5) needles and MC, cast on 14 sts.
Beg with a k row, work 44 rows in st st.
Cast off.

ARMS
With 3¾ mm (UK 9/US 5) needles and MC, cast on 14 sts.
Beg with a k row, work 44 rows in st st.
Cast off.

BODY
With 3¾ mm (UK 9/US 5) needles and MC, cast on 17 sts for neck edge.
P 1 row.
Next row: K1, [m1, k1] 7 times, k2, [m1, k1] 7 times. (31 sts.)
Work 5 rows.

Next row: [K5, m1] 3 times, k1, [m1, k5] 3 times. (37 sts.)
Work 3 rows.
Next row: [K6, m1] 3 times, k1, [m1, k6] 3 times. (43 sts.)
Work 27 rows.
Next row: [K8, skpo] twice, k3, [k2tog, k8] twice. (39 sts.)
P 1 row.
Next row: [K7, skpo] twice, k3, [k2tog, k7] twice. (35 sts.)
P 1 row.
Cast off.

HEAD
With 3¾ mm (UK 9/US 5) needles and MC, cast on 13 sts.
P 1 row.
Next row: K1, [m1, k1] to end. (25 sts.)
P 1 row.
Next row: K1, [m1, k2] to end. (37 sts.)
St st 3 rows.
Next row: [K9, m1] twice, k1, [m1, k9] twice. (41 sts.)
P 1 row.
Next row: K20, m1, k1, m1, k20. (43 sts.)
St st 15 rows.
Next row: [K8, skpo] twice, k3, [k2tog, k8] twice. (39 sts.)
P 1 row.
Next row: [K7, skpo] twice, k3, [k2tog, k7] twice. (35 sts.)
P 1 row.
Next row: [K6, skpo] twice, k3, [k2tog, k6] twice. (31 sts.)
St st 3 rows.
Next row: K1, [k2tog, k1] to end. (21 sts.)
P 1 row.
Next row: K1, [k2tog] to end. (11 sts.)
Next row: P1, [p2tog] to end. (6 sts.)
Break off yarn, thread through rem sts, pull up tightly and fasten off securely.

MUZZLE

With 3¾ mm (UK 9/US 5) needles and A, cast on 32 sts.

Beg with a k row work 6 rows st st.

Next row: K2tog, [k1, k2tog] to end. (21 sts.)

P 1 row.

Next row: K1, [k2tog] to end. (11 sts.)

Break yarn, thread through rem sts, pull up tightly and fasten off securely.

EYE PIECE

With 3¾ mm (UK 9/US 5) needles and A, cast on 19 sts.

Beg with a k row work 6 rows st st.

Next row: K1, [k2tog] to end. (10 sts.)

Break yarn, thread through rem sts, pull up tightly and fasten off securely.

FEET

With 3¾ mm (UK 9/US 5) needles and A, cast on 8 sts.

Beg with a p row, work 3 rows st st.

Inc 1 st at each end of next row and 2 foll alt rows, then on foll 4th row. (16 sts.)

St st 3 rows.

Next row: K2tog, k3, turn, leave rem sts.

P 1 row.

Next row: K2tog, k2.

Next row: P2tog, p1.

K2tog and fasten off. Rejoin yarn to inside of rem sts, k to last 2 sts, k2tog. (10 sts.)

P 1 row.

Next row: K2tog, k to last 2 sts, k2tog.

Cast off rem 8 sts.

Make another piece exactly the same, then make a further two pieces, reversing shapings, by reading p for k and k for p.

HANDS

Work as given for feet.

TAIL

With 3¾ mm (UK 9/US 5) needles and MC, cast on 9 sts.

Beg with a K row, work in st st for 48 rows.

Next row: K2tog, k5, k2tog.

St st 3 rows.

Next row: K2tog, k3, k2tog.

P 1 row.

Next row: K2tog, k1, k2tog.

K3tog and fasten off.

Break yarn, thread through rem sts, pull up tightly and fasten off securely.

EARS

With 3¾ mm (UK 9/US 5) needles and MC, cast on 11 sts.

Beg with a K row, work in st st for 6 rows.

Dec 1 st at each end of next and foll alt row. (7 sts.)

Work 1 row.

Cast off.

Make another piece using MC, then make a further 2 pieces using A.

TO MAKE UP

Join outside edges of feet to make a pair. Join cast-on edge to cast-on edge of legs. Join leg seam, stuff and join top seam.

Fold sides of cast-off edge of body to centre and sew it together, join back seam. Stuff firmly. Gather neck edge, pull up and secure. Join outside edges of hands to make a pair. Join cast-on edge to cast-on edge of arms. Join arm seam, stuff and join top seam. Attach arms and legs to body.

Join head seam, leaving an opening, stuff and join opening. Attach to body. Join eye piece seam, sew to head. Join muzzle seam, sew to head, stuffing lightly. Sew pairs of ears together, leaving cast-on edges open, then sew ears to sides of head.

Embroider eyes and nostrils in satin stitch and mouth in stem stitch using Black.

Pig

This adorable piglet is a perfect size for a little friend to take on a trip to the farm. Knitted in soft baby pink wool, this faithful piglet can easily be tucked under a child's arm.

SKILL LEVEL 2

MEASUREMENTS
Approximately 16 cm (6¼ in) tall

MATERIALS
- 2 x 50 g balls of Jaeger Baby Merino DK in Pale Pink
- Oddments of Jaeger Baby Merino DK in Black
- Pair 3¼ mm (UK 10/US 3) knitting needles
- Washable toy stuffing

ABBREVIATIONS
See page 14.

TENSION
24 sts and 32 rows to 10 cm (4 in) measured over stocking stitch using 3¼ mm (UK 10/US 3) needles.

UPPER BODY
With 3¼ mm (UK 10/US 3) needles and Pale Pink, cast on 76 sts.
K 1 row.
Shape back legs
Cont in st st.
Cast on 3 sts at beg of next 4 rows and 6 sts at beg of foll 2 rows. (100 sts.)
St st 12 rows.
Cast off 6 sts at beg of next 2 rows and 3 sts at beg of foll 4 rows. (76 sts.)
St st 35 rows.
Shape front legs
Cast on 12 sts at beg of next 2 rows. (100 sts.)
St st 10 rows.
Cast off 12 sts at beg of next 2 rows. (76 sts.)
St st 10 rows.

Shape head
Next row: K16, [k2tog tbl, k9] twice, [k9, k2tog] twice, k16.
St st 3 rows.
Next row: K16, [k2tog tbl, k8] twice, [k8, k2tog] twice, k16.
St st 3 rows.
Place marker at each end of last row.
Next row: K16, [k2tog tbl, k7] twice, [k7, k2tog] twice, k16. (64 sts.)
P 1 row.
Cont in this way, dec 4 sts as set on 5 foll alt rows. (44 sts.)
St st 9 rows.
Next row: K6, [k twice in next st, k5] 6 times, k2. (50 sts.)
P 1 row.
Cast off.

UNDERBODY

With 3¼ mm (UK 10/US 3) needles and Pale Pink, cast on 3 sts.

K 1 row.

Cont in st st, inc 1 st at each end of next 3 rows and 4 foll alt rows. (17 sts.)

St st 6 rows.

Dec 1 st at each end of next row and 2 foll alt rows. (11 sts.)

St st 5 rows.

Mark each end of last row.

Shape back legs

Cast on 3 sts at beg of next 6 rows and 6 sts at beg of foll 2 rows. (41 sts.)

Next row: K15, k2tog tbl, k7, k2tog, k15.

St st 2 rows.

Next row: P14, p2tog, p7, p2tog tbl, p14.

St st 2 rows.

Next row: K13, k2tog tbl, k7, k2tog, k13.

St st 2 rows.

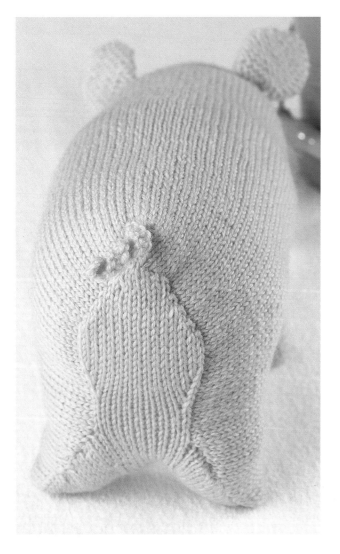

Next row: P12, p2tog, p7, p2tog tbl, p12.

St st 2 rows.

Cast off 3 sts at beg of next 2 rows.

Next row: Cast off 3 sts, k until there are 5 sts on right needle, k2tog tbl, k7, k2tog, k5.

Cast off 3 sts at beg of next 3 rows. (13 sts.)

St st 34 rows.

Shape front legs

Cast on 12 sts at beg of next 2 rows. (37 sts.)

St st 10 rows.

Cast off 12 sts at beg of next 2 rows. (13 sts.)

St st 8 rows.

Dec 1 st at each end of the next and 4 foll alt rows.

P 1 row.

Cast off.

SNOUT

With 3¼ mm (UK 10/US 3) needles and Pale Pink, cast on 3 sts.

K 1 row.

Cont in g st, inc 1 st at each end of the next 3 rows and 3 foll alt rows. K 7 rows.

Dec 1 st at each end of next and 2 foll alt rows, then on 3 foll rows.

K 1 row.

Cast off.

EARS (make 2)

With 3¼ mm (UK 10/US 3) needles and Pale Pink, cast on 17 sts.

K 6 rows.

Dec 1 st at each end of the next row, 2 foll 4th rows, then 4 foll alt rows.

K 1 row.

K3tog and fasten off.

TAIL

With 3¼ mm (UK 10/US 3) needles and Pale Pink, cast on 20 sts loosely. Cast off tightly.

TO MAKE UP

Join seam from cast-off edge to maker. Sew in snout. Leaving a gap, join upperbody to underbody, matching legs and continue back seam to centre of cast-on sts. Stuff and close opening.

Fold sides of ear to centre at cast-on edge and secure. Sew on ears and tail.

Embroider eyes and nostrils in satin stitch using Black.

Embroider mouth in stem stitch using Black.

Zebra

Go wild with this crazy striped zebra and imagine being in the hot, sunny grasslands of Africa. This simple, yet effective toy is knitted in bold black and white double knitting.

MEASUREMENTS
Approximately 32 cm (12½ in) high

MATERIALS
- 1 x 50 g ball of Jaeger Matchmaker Merino DK in Black
- 1 x 50 g ball of Jaeger Matchmaker Merino DK in White
- Oddment of brown yarn for facial features
- Pair of 3¼ mm (UK 10/UK 3) knitting needles
- Washable toy stuffing

ABBREVIATIONS
See page 14.

TENSION
24 sts and 32 rows to 10 cm (4 in) measured over stocking stitch using 3¼ mm (UK 10/US 3) needles.

LEGS
With 3¼ mm (UK 10/US 3) needles and Black, cast on 20 sts.
Beg with a K row, cont in st st, working 2 rows Black, then stripes of 4 rows White and 4 rows Black.
Work 6 rows.
Dec 1 st at end of next row.
Work 9 rows.
Dec 1 st at beg of next row.
Work 21 rows.
Dec 1 st at each end of next 3 rows.
Cast off rem 12 sts.

ARMS
With 3¼ mm (UK 10/US 3) needles and White, cast on 7 sts.
Beg with a K row, cont in st st, working 2 rows White, then stripes of 4 rows Black, and 4 rows White.
Work 1 row.

Inc 1 st at each end of next 4 rows. (15 sts.)
Work 7 rows.
Dec 1 st at end of next row.
Work 9 rows.
Dec 1 st at beg of next row.
Work 11 rows.
Shape for hand
Cont in Black only.
Work 1 row.
Inc 1 st at each end of next 2 rows. (17 sts.)
Work 5 rows.
Next row: K1, skpo, k3, k2tog, k1, skpo, k3, k2tog, k1. (13 sts.)
Next row: P.
Next row: K1, skpo, k1, k2tog, k1, skpo, k1, k2tog, k1. (9 sts.)
Next row: P.
Next row: K1, sl 1, k2tog, psso, k1, sl 1, k2tog, psso, k1. Break yarn, thread through rem 5 sts and fasten off.

BACK BODY
With 3¼ mm (UK 10/US 3) needles and Black, cast on 6 sts.
Beg with a K row, cont in st st, working 2 rows Black, then stripes of 4 rows White and 4 rows Black.
Work 2 rows.
Next row: K1, * m1, k1; rep from * to end. (11 sts.)
Work 3 rows.
Next row: K1, [m1, k2] 5 times. (16 sts.)
Work 3 rows.
Next row: K2, [m1, k3] 4 times, m1, k2. (21 sts.)
Work 3 rows.
Next row: K3, [m1, k4] 4 times, m1, k2. (26 sts.)
Work 23 rows.
Next row: K1, [k2tog, k3] 5 times. (21 sts.)
Work 3 rows.
Next row: K1, [k2tog, k2] 5 times. (16 sts.)
Work 3 rows.
Next row: K1, [k2tog, k1] 5 times. (11 sts.)
Work 3 rows.
Cast off rem 11 sts.

FRONT BODY

With 3¼ mm (UK 10/US 3) needles and Black, cast on 6 sts.

Beg with a K row, cont in st st, working 2 rows Black, then stripes of 4 rows White and 4 rows Black.

Work 2 rows.

Next row: K1, [m1, k1] 5 times. (11 sts.)

Work 3 rows.

Next row: K1, [m1, k2] 5 times. (16 sts.)

Work 3 rows.

Next row: K2, [m1, k2] 7 times. (23 sts.)

Work 3 rows.

Next row: K2, [m1, k3] 7 times. (30 sts.)

Work 23 rows.

Next row: K2, [k2tog, k6] 3 times, k2tog, k2. (26 sts.)

Work 3 rows.

Next row: K2, k2tog, k5, k2tog, k4, k2tog, k5, k2tog, k2. (22 sts.)

Work 3 rows.

Next row: K2, [k2tog, k1] 6 times, k2. (16 sts.)

Work 3 rows.

Cast off rem 16 sts.

HEAD

With 3¼ mm (UK 10/US 3) needles and White, cast on 7 sts.

P 1 row.

Next row: K1, [m1, k1] to end.

Rep the last 2 rows once more. (25 sts.)

P 1 row.

Next row: K3, [m1, k2] to end. (36 sts.)

P 1 row.

Next row: K3, [m1, k3] to end. (47 sts.)

P 1 row.

Next row: K3, [m1, k4] to end. (58 sts.)

Work 3 rows in st st.

Next row: K48, turn.

Next row: P38, turn.

Next row: K34, turn.

Next row: P30, turn.

Next row: K26, turn.

Next row: P22, turn.

Next row: K18, turn.

Next row: P14, turn.

Next row: K10, turn.

Next row: P6, turn.
Next row: K to end.
Work 7 rows in st st.
Next row: K10, k2tog, k6, skpo, k18, k2tog, k6, skpo, k10. (54 sts.)
Next row: P to end.
Next row: K9, k2tog, k6, skpo, k16, k2tog, k6, skpo, k9.
Next row: P to end.
Next row: K8, k2tog, k6, skpo, k14, k2tog, k6, skpo, k8.

Next row: P to end.
Next row: K7, k2tog, k6, skpo, k12, k2tog, k6, skpo, k7.
Next row: P to end.
Next row: K6, k2tog, k6, skpo, k10, k2tog, k6, skpo, k6.
Next row: P to end.
Next row: K5, k2tog, k6, skpo, k8, k2tog, k6, skpo, k5. (34 sts.)
Change to Black.
Next row: P to end.
Next row: K4, k2tog, k6, skpo, k6, k2tog, k6, skpo, k4.
Work 3 rows.
Next row: K3, k2tog, k6, skpo, k4, k2tog, k6, skpo, k3.
Work 3 rows.
Next row: K2, k2tog, k6, skpo, k2, k2tog, k6, skpo, k2. (22 sts.)
Work 3 rows.
Next row: K4, skpo, k2tog, k6, skpo, k2tog, k4.
Work 1 row.
Next row: K3, skpo, k2tog, k4, skpo, k2tog, k3.
Work 1 row.
Cast off rem 14 sts.

EARS (make 2 pairs)
With 3¼ mm (UK 10/US 3) needles and White, cast on 12 sts.
Work 8 rows in st st.
Change to Black.
Dec 1 st at each end of the next 5 rows.
Work 2 tog and fasten off.

TO MAKE UP
Join leg and arm seams, stuff. Join side and cast-on edges of body, stuff. Join seam of head.
With seam to centre of cast-off edge, join "nose" seam, stuff. Join head to body.
Attach arms and legs to body. Sew pairs of ears, stuff lightly, sew to top of head along line formed by turning rows.
With Black work a row of loops between ears.
Embroider French knots for eyes in Black and French knots for nostrils in Brown.
Using Brown, embroider mouth in stem stitch.
For tail, make a twisted cord in Black, 8 cm (3 in) long. Knot one end and trim to form a short tassel.
Attach the other end to back of body.

FRONT LEG SOLES (make 2)

With 3¼ mm (UK10/US 3) needles and Brown, cast on
6 sts. K 1 row. Cont in st st, inc 1 st at each end of
next 2 rows. Work 1 row. Inc 1 st at each end of next
row and foll 3rd row. (14 sts.)
St st 3 rows. Dec 1 st at each end of next row and foll
3rd row. Work 1 row. Dec 1 st at each end of next 2
rows. (6 sts.)
Cast off.

RIGHT SIDE HEAD

With 3¼ mm (UK10/US 3) needles and Brown, cast
on 13 sts for neck edge. K 1 row. Mark end of
last row.

Shape neck and back edge: 1st row: P to last st, inc.
2nd row: Inc, k to last st, inc.
3rd row: P to last st, inc.
4th row: Inc, k to end. Rep these 4 rows, twice more,
then work 1st and 2nd row again. (31 sts.)
Mark beg of last row. St st 3 rows. Inc 1 st at end of
next row. (32 sts.) Work 1 row.
Shape chin: Cast on 3 sts at beg of next row and 7 foll
alt rows. (56 sts.)
Mark beg of last row. St st 3 rows.
Shape top: Cast off 6 sts at beg of next row and foll
alt row, then 12 sts at beg of 2 foll alt rows. (20 sts.)
Cast off rem sts.

LEFT SIDE HEAD

Work as given for Right Side Head, reversing shapings by reading p for k and k for p.

TOP GUSSET

With 3¼ mm (UK10/US 3) needles and Brown, cast on 12 sts. Beg with a k row, work in st st, inc 1 st at each end of 3rd row, foll 4th row and foll 6th row. (18 sts.) St st 4 rows.

Using separate small balls of yarn for each coloured area and twisting yarns together on wrong side at join, work as follows:

1st row: P15 Brown, 3 Cream.
2nd row: With Cream, inc, k4, with Brown, k12, inc.

3rd row: P12 Brown, 8 Cream.
4th row: K9 Cream, 11 Brown.
5th row: P10 Brown, 10 Cream.
6th row: K11 Cream, 9 Brown.
7th row: With Brown, inc, p8, with Cream, p10, inc.
8th row: K13 Cream, 9 Brown.
9th row: With Brown, inc, p8, with Cream, p12, inc.
10th row: K14 Cream, 10 Brown.
11th row: With Brown, inc, p9, with Cream, p13, inc.
12th row: K15 Cream, 11 Brown.
13th row: With Brown, inc, p10, with Cream, p14, inc.
14th row: With Cream, inc, k15, with Brown, k11, inc.
15th row: With Brown, inc, p12, with Cream, p16, inc.
16th row: With Cream, inc, k17, with Brown, k13, inc.

17th row: P15 Brown, 19 Cream.

18th row: K18 Cream, 16 Brown.

19th row: P16 Brown, 18 Cream.

20th row: With Cream, inc, k16, with Brown, k16, inc.

21st row: P18 Brown, 18 Cream.

22nd row: K17 Cream, 19 Brown.

23rd row: P20 Brown, 16 Cream.

24th row: With Cream, inc, k14, with Brown, k20, inc. (38 sts.)

25th row: P24 Brown, 14 Cream.

26th row: K12 Cream, 26 Brown.

27th row: P28 Brown, 10 Cream.

28th row: K6 Cream, 32 Brown.

Cont in Brown only, st st 15 rows. Mark each end of last row. Dec 1 st at each end of next 2 rows. (34 sts.)

Next row: Dec, k10, [skpo] twice, k2, [k2tog] twice, k10, dec. Dec 1 st at each end of next row. (26 sts.)

Next row: Dec, k6, [skpo] twice, k2, [k2tog] twice, k6, dec. Dec 1 st at each end of next row. (18 sts.)

Next row: Dec, k2, [skpo] twice, k2, [k2tog] twice, k2, dec. Dec 1 st at each end of next row. (10 sts.) Cast off.

UNDERCHIN GUSSET

With 3¼ mm (UK10/US 3) needles and Brown, cast on 16 sts. Cont in st st, inc 1 st at each end of 7th row and 4 foll 6th rows. (26 sts.) St st 13 rows. Dec 1 st at each end of next 8 rows. (10 sts.) Cast off.

EARS (make 4)

With 3¼ mm (UK10/US 3) needles and Brown, cast on 12 sts. Cont in st st, inc 1 st at each end of 5th row and 5 foll 6th rows. (24 sts.) St st 21 rows. Dec 1 st at each end of next 4 rows. (16 sts.) Cast off.

NOSE

With 3¼ mm (UK10/US 3) needles and Black, cast on 8 sts. K 1 row. Cont in st st, inc 1 st at each end of next 4 rows. (16 sts.) St st 11 rows. Dec 1 st at each end of next 4 rows. (8 sts.) Cast off.

EYES (make 2)

With 3¼ mm (UK10/US 3) needles and Black, cast on 3 sts. K 1 row. Cont in st st, inc 1 st at each end of next 2 rows. (7 sts.) St st 4 rows. Dec 1 st at each end of next 2 rows. (3 sts.) Cast off.

LEFT SIDE TAIL

With 3¼ mm (UK10/US 3) needles and Brown, cast on 19 sts. Beg with a k row, st st 2 rows.

1st row: K to last 2 sts, dec. P 1 row.

3rd row: Inc, k to last 2 sts, dec. P 1 row. Rep these 4 rows, 3 times. (15 sts.)

Next row: K to last 2 sts, dec. P 1 row. Rep last 2 rows, 4 times more. (10 sts.) Cast off.

RIGHT SIDE TAIL

Work as given for Left Side Tail, reversing shapings by reading p for k and k for p.

TAIL TOP

With 3¼ mm (UK10/US 3) needles and Black, cast on 10 sts. K 1 row, p 1 row.

Next row: Inc in each st to end. (20 sts.) P 1 row.

Next row: [K1, inc] to end. (30 sts.) St st 3 rows.

Next row: [K2, inc] to end. (40 sts.) St st 5 rows.

Next row: [K2, dec] to end. (30 sts.) St st 3 rows.

Next row: [K1, dec] to end. (20 sts.) P 1 row.

Next row: [Dec] to end. (10 sts.) Break off yarn, leaving a long end. Thread end through sts, pull up and secure.

TO MAKE UP

Join body pieces together, leaving cast-on and cast-off edges of legs open and small opening at side. Sew in soles. Stuff body firmly and close opening. Join head sides together along back edge. Place top of this seam to centre of cast-on edge of top gusset and, matching markers on gusset to markers at top of chin shaping on sides, sew in top gusset.

Line up cast-on edge of underchin gusset with markers at beginning of chin shaping on sides and sew in underchin gusset.

Stuff head firmly, position on body near front legs and stitch in place.

Join paired ear pieces together, position on head and sew in place. Run a gathering thread around nose piece and pull up lightly, stuff the nose, pull the thread tightly and secure. Position nose on head and stitch in place.

Run a gathering thread around each eye piece, pull up tightly and secure. Position on head and stitch in place.

Join tail pieces together, leaving cast-on and cast-off edge free. Join top tail along row ends, stuff firmly and sew to cast-off edge of tail, then stuff tail. Sew cast-on edge of tail to body.

Small teddy bear

Every bear needs a friend and this little teddy is well worth
your affection. Because of his size, he can be carried
everywhere in a pocket or bag.

SKILL LEVEL 3

MEASUREMENTS
Teddy: approximately 20 cm (8 in) high
Scarf: 38 x 2.5 cm (15 x 1 in)

MATERIALS
- 1 x 50 g ball of Rowan Kid Classic in Light Natural (MC)
- 1 x 50 g ball of Rowan Kid Classic in Caramel (A)
- Oddments of Patons Diploma Gold DK in Blue, Yellow and Red
- Pair of 3¼ mm (UK 10/US 3) knitting needles
- 3.25 mm (UK 10/US D3) crochet hook
- Washable toy stuffing
- Brown embroidery thread for facial features

ABBREVIATIONS
See page 14.

TENSION
Teddy: 24 sts and 32 rows to 10 cm (4 in) measured over stocking stitch using 3¼ mm (UK 10/US 3) needles.

BEAR
LEGS (make 2)
With 3¼ mm (UK 10/US 3) needles and MC, cast on 26 sts.
Beg with a K row, work 5 rows st st.
Next row: P13, turn.
Work on this set of sts only.
Dec 1 st at beg of next row and foll alt row, then at end of next row. (10 sts.)
Break off yarn and rejoin at inside edge to second set of sts, p to end.
Dec 1 st at end of next row and foll alt row, then at beg of next row. (10 sts.)
K 1 row across all sts. (20 sts.)

Work 18 rows.
Next row: P10, turn and work on this set of sts only.
Dec 1 st at each end of next 2 rows. (6 sts.)
Cast off.
Rejoin yarn to rem sts and complete to match first side.

SOLES (make 2)
With 3¼ mm (UK 10/US 3) needles and A, cast on 3 sts.
Beg with a k row cont in st st.
K 1 row.
Inc 1 st at each end of the next 2 rows and foll alt row. (9 sts.)
Work 6 rows straight.
Dec 1 st at each end of the next row, foll alt row, then on foll row. (3 sts.)
Work 1 row.
Cast off.

ARMS (make 2)
* With 3¼ mm (UK 10/US 3) needles and MC, cast on 4 sts.
Beg with a k row work 2 rows in st st.
Inc 1 st at each end of next and foll alt row.
Work 1 row *.
Break off yarn.
Rep from * to *.
K 1 row across all sts. (16 sts.)
Inc 1 st at each end of 2nd row and foll 4th row. (20 sts.)
Work 15 rows straight.
Next row: K10, turn.
Work on this set of sts only.
Dec 1 st at each end of next 2 rows. (6 sts.)
Work 1 row.
Cast off.
Rejoin yarn to rem sts and complete as first side.

BODY (make 2)

* With 3¼ mm (UK 10/US 3) needles and MC, cast on 3 sts.

Beg with a k row cont in st st.

Work 1 row.

Inc 1 st at each end of the next 2 rows and 2 foll alt rows. (11 sts.) *.

Break off yarn.

Rep from * to *.

P 1 row across both sets of sts. (22 sts.)

Work 12 rows straight.

Dec 1 st at each end of next row, and 2 foll 3rd rows, then on foll alt row. (14 sts.)

Work 1 row.

Cast off.

BACK HEAD

With 3¼ mm (UK 10/US 3) needles and MC, cast on 3 sts.

K 1 row.

Cont in st st, inc 1 st at each end of next 2 rows, then at end of foll 3 rows. (10 sts.)

Work 1 row.

Inc 1 st at beg of next row. (11 sts.)

K 1 row.

Break off yarn.

Using MC cast on 3 sts.

K 1 row.

Cont in st st, inc 1 st at each end of next 2 rows, then at beg of foll 3 rows. (10 sts.)

Work 1 row.

Inc 1 st at end of next row. (11 sts.)

K 1 row.

P 1 row across all sts. (22 sts.)

Work 6 rows straight.

Next row: K11, turn.

Work on this set of sts only.

Dec 1 st at each end of next row.

Work 1 row.

Dec 1 st at end of next 3 rows.

Mark end of last row.

Dec 1 st at each end of next row. (4 sts.)

Work 1 row.

Cast off.

Rejoin at inside edge to rem sts, k to end.

Dec 1 st at each end of next row.

Work 1 row.

Dec 1 st at beg of next 3 rows.

Mark beg of last row.

Dec 1 st at each end of next row. (4 sts.)

Work 1 row.

Cast off.

HEAD GUSSET

With 3¼ mm (UK 10/US 3) needles and MC, cast on 11 sts.

Work 4 rows st st.

Dec 1 st at each end of next row and foll alt row, then on foll row.

Work 2 rows.

Dec 1 st at each end of next row.

Work 1 row.

Work 3 tog and fasten off.

RIGHT SIDE OF HEAD

With 3¼ mm (UK 10/US 3) needles and MC, cast on 6 sts.

Beg with a k row, cont in st st.

Work 1 row.

Inc 1 st at beg of next row.

Inc 1 st at each end of next row and beg of foll 4 rows, then at end of next row.

Inc 1 st at beg of next row. (15 sts.)

Work 5 rows straight.

Mark end of last row.

Cast off 2 sts at beg of next row.

Dec 1 st at end of next row and at beg of foll row. (11 sts.)

* Dec 1 st at each end of next row, then at beg of foll row *.

Rep from * to *. (5 sts.)

Work 1 row.

Mark beg of last row. Cast off.

LEFT SIDE OF HEAD

Work as given for Right side of head, reversing shapings.

EARS (make 2 in MC and 2 in A)

With 3¼ mm (UK 10/US 3) needles, cast on 6 sts.

Work 3 rows st st.

Dec 1 st at each end of next 2 rows.

Cast off.

TO MAKE UP

Note: Purl side of knitting is used as right side.

Join instep, top and inner back leg seams leaving an opening.

Sew in soles. Stuff and close opening. Join arm seams, leaving an opening. Stuff and close opening. Join centre seam on each body piece, join body pieces together, leaving cast-off edge open.

Stuff and gather open edge, pull up and secure.

Join sides of head from cast-on edge to first marker.

Sew in head gusset, placing point at centre front seam and cast-on edge in line with second markers on sides of head. Join centre seams of back head, then sew to front head, matching markers and leaving cast-on edge open.

Stuff and gather open edge, pull up and secure. Sew head to body.

Attach yarn about 1 cm (½ in) below top of one arm, thread through body at shoulder position, then attach other arm, pull yarn tightly and thread through body again in same place, then attach to first arm and fasten off.

Attach legs in same way. Join paired ear pieces together and sew them in place.

Using brown embroidery thread, embroider eyes and nose in satin stitch and mouth in straight stitch.

SCARF

With 3¼ mm (UK 10/US 3) needles and Blue, cast on 7 sts and work in g st as follows:

2 rows Blue, 2 rows Yellow, 2 rows Red.

These 6 rows form rep of patt, cont in stripe patt until scarf meas 38 cm (15 in), ending with 2 rows Blue.

Cast off.

Make fringe of 5 tassels at each end of scarf, using Blue (see page 13).

Large teddy bear

Cute and cuddly pretty much sums up this guy: all he wants is care and attention, but careful – you may fall in love with him before the children can get him!

SKILL LEVEL 3

MEASUREMENTS
Approximately 36 cm (14 in) high

MATERIALS
- 2 x 50 g balls of Rowan Kid Classic in Light Natural (MC)
- 1 x 50 g ball of Rowan Kid Classic in Caramel (A)
- 2 x 50 g balls of Patons Diploma Gold DK in Red
- Pair each of 3¼ mm (UK 10/US 3) and 4 mm (UK 8/US 6) knitting needles
- Washable toy stuffing
- Brown embroidery thread for facial features

ABBREVIATIONS
See page 14.

TENSION
Teddy: 24 sts and 32 rows to 10 cm (4 in) measured over stocking stitch using 3¼ mm (UK 10/US 3) needles.
Sweater: 22 sts and 30 rows to 10 cm (4 in) measured over stocking stitch using 4 mm (UK 8/US 6) needles.

BEAR
LEGS (make 2)
With 3¼ mm (UK 10/US 3) needles and MC, cast on 50 sts.
Beg with a K row, work 10 rows st st.
Next row: K25, turn.
Work on this set of sts only.
Dec 1 st at beg of next row and 3 foll alt rows, then at end of next row and beg of foll row. (19 sts.)
Work 1 row.
Break off yarn and rejoin at inside edge to second set of sts, k to end.
Dec 1 st at end of next row and 3 foll alt rows, then at

beg of next row and end of foll row. (19 sts.)
Work 1 row.
P 1 row across all sts. (38 sts.)
Work 27 rows.
Next row: P19, turn and work on this set of sts only.
Dec 1 st at each end of next row and 2 foll alt rows, then on 2 foll rows. (9 sts.)
Work 1 row.
Cast off.
Rejoin yarn to rem sts and complete to match first side.

SOLES (make 2)
With 3¼ mm (UK 10/US 3) needles and A, cast on 5 sts.
Beg with a k row cont in st st.
K 1 row.
Inc 1 st at each end of the next 3 rows and foll alt row. (13 sts.)
Work 11 rows straight.
Dec 1 st at each end of the next row, foll 4th row and on foll alt row, then at each end of the next 2 rows. (3 sts.)
Cast off.

ARMS (make 2)

* With 3¼ mm (UK 10/US 3) needles and MC, cast on
8 sts.
Beg with a k row work 2 rows in st st.
Inc 1 st at each end of next and foll alt row.
Work 1 row *.
Inc 1 st at beg of next row.
Work 1 row.
Inc 1 st at each end of foll row. (15 sts.)
Work 1 row.
Break off yarn.
Rep from * to *.
Inc 1 st at end of next row.
Work 1 row.
Inc 1 st at each end of foll row. (15 sts.)
Work 1 row.
K 1 row across all sts. (30 sts.)
Inc 1 st at each end of 2nd row and 3 foll 6th rows.
(38 sts.)

Work 20 rows straight.
Next row: P19, turn.
Work on this set of sts only.
Dec 1 st at each end of next row and 2 foll alt rows,
then on 2 foll rows. (9 sts.)
Work 1 row.
Cast off.
Rejoin yarn to rem sts and complete as first side.

BODY (make 2)

* With 3¼ mm (UK 10/US 3) needles and MC, cast on
7 sts.
Beg with a k row cont in st st.
Work 1 row.
Inc 1 st at each end of the next 2 rows and 5 foll alt
rows. (21 sts.)
Work 1 row *.
Break off yarn.
Rep from * to *.
K 1 row across both sets of sts. (42 sts.)
Work 25 rows straight.
Dec 1 st at each end of next row, 2 foll 4th rows and
3 foll alt rows, then on every row until 20 sts rem.
Cast off.

BACK HEAD

With 3¼ mm (UK 10/US 3) needles and MC, cast on
7 sts.
K 1 row.
Cont in st st, inc 1 st at each end of next 2 rows, then
at end of foll 5 rows. (16 sts.)
Work 1 row.
Inc 1 st at beg of next 2 rows. (18 sts.)
Break off yarn.
Using MC, cast on 7 sts.
K 1 row.
Cont in st st, inc one st at each end of next 2 rows,
then at beg of foll 5 rows.
Work 1 row.
Inc 1 st at end of next 2 rows. (18 sts.)
P 1 row across all sts. (36 sts.)
Work 22 rows straight.
Next row: K2tog, k16, turn.
Work on this set of sts only.
Dec 1 st at each end of 2 foll 3rd rows, then foll alt
row. (11 sts.)
Mark beg of last row.
Dec 1 st at end of next row, each end of foll row and
at end of next row. (7 sts.)
Cast off.
Rejoin at inside edge to rem sts, k to last 2 sts, k2tog.

Dec 1 st at each end of 2 foll 3rd rows, then foll alt row. Mark end of last row.
Dec 1 st at beg of next row, each end of foll row and at beg of next row. (7 sts.)
Cast off.

HEAD GUSSET

With 3¼ mm (UK 10/US 3) needles and MC, cast on 20 sts.
Work 10 rows in st st.
Dec 1 st at each end of next row and 3 foll 4th rows, then on 3 foll alt rows. (6 sts.)
Work 3 rows.
Dec 1 st at each end of next 2 rows.
Work 2 tog and fasten off.

RIGHT SIDE OF HEAD

With 3¼ mm (UK 10/US 3) needles and MC, cast on 10 sts.
Beg with a k row, cont in st st.
Work 1 row.
Inc 1 st at beg of next row.
Inc 1 st at each end of next row and beg of foll 6 rows, then at end of next row. (20 sts.)
Inc 1 st at each end of next row. (22 sts.)

Inc 1 st at end of next row and at same edge on foll 3 rows. (26 sts.)
Work 11 rows straight.
Mark end of last row.
Cast off 2 sts at beg of next row. (24 sts.)
Dec 1 st at end of next row and and at same edge on foll 6 rows. (17 sts.)
Dec 1 st at each end of next row, then at end of foll row.
Dec 1 st at each end of foll alt row. (12 sts.)
Work 1 row.
Dec 1 st at end of next 3 rows. (9 sts.)
Work 1 row.
Mark end of last row.
Cast off.

LEFT SIDE OF HEAD

Work as given for Right side of head, reversing shapings.

EARS (make 2 in MC and 2 in A)

With 3¼ mm (UK 10/US 3) needles cast on 13 sts.
Work 5 rows in st st.
Dec 1 st at each end of next 5 rows. (3 sts.)
Cast off.

TO MAKE UP

Note: Purl side of knitting is used as right side.

Join instep, top and inner back leg seams leaving an opening.

Sew in soles. Stuff and close opening. Join arm seams, leaving an opening.

Stuff and close opening. Join centre seam on each body piece, join body pieces together, leaving cast-off edge open.

Stuff and gather open edge, pull up and secure. Join sides of head from cast-on edge to first marker.

Sew in head gusset, placing point at centre front seam and cast-on edge in line with second markers on sides of head.

Join centre seams of back head, then sew to front head, matching markers and leaving cast-on edge open.

Stuff and gather open edge, pull up and secure. Sew head to body.

Attach yarn about 1 cm (½ in) below top of one arm, thread through body at shoulder position, then attach other arm, pull yarn tightly and thread through body again in same place, then attach to first arm and fasten off.

Attach legs in same way. Join paired ear pieces together and sew them in place.

Using brown embroidery thread, embroider eyes and nose in satin stitch and mouth in straight stitch.

SWEATER
BACK

With 3¼ mm (UK 10/US 3) needles and Red, cast on 42 sts.

Beg with a k row, work 4 rows in st st.

Change to 4 mm (UK 8/US 6) needles.

Beg with a k row, work in st st throughout, until Back meas 16 cm (6 in) from beg, ending with a WS row.

Shape shoulders

Cast off 10 sts at beg of next 2 rows.

Leave rem 22 sts on a holder.

FRONT

Work as for Back until work meas 13 cm (5 in) from beg, ending with a WS row.

Shape neck

Next row: K15, turn.

Work on this set of sts only.

Dec 1 st at neck edge on every row until 10 sts rem. Work straight until Front matches Back to shoulder shaping, ending at armhole edge.

Shape shoulder

Cast off 10 sts at beg of next row.

With RS facing, rejoin yarn to rem sts, sl centre 12 sts on to a holder, k to end.

Complete to match first side, reversing shapings, work an extra row before start of shoulder shaping.

SLEEVES

With 3¼ mm (UK 10/US 3) needles and Red, cast on 28 sts.

Beg with a k row, work 4 rows in st st.

Change to 4 mm (UK 8/US 6) needles.

Beg with a k row, work in st st throughout, shaping sides by inc 1 st at each end of 3rd and every foll 4th row until there are 34 sts.

Cont straight until Sleeve meas 11 cm (4½ in), ending after a WS row.

NECKBAND

Join right shoulder seam.

With 3¼ mm (UK 10/US 3) needles and RS facing, k up 9 sts down left front neck, k centre 12 sts, k up 9 sts up right front neck, k 22 sts back neck sts. (52 sts.)

Beg with a p row, work 9 rows in rev st st. Cast off.

TO MAKE UP

Join left shoulder seam, reversing seam on st st roll.

Sew on sleeves, reversing seam on st st roll.

Join side and sleeve seams, reversing seam on st st roll.

Girl rag doll

This bright and cheerful girl rag doll has all the appeal of a traditional old-fashioned doll and yet is still a great toy for any little girl. You can knit a whole wardrobe for her by altering the colours and textures of the jumper, skirt and shoes.

SKILL LEVEL 3

MEASUREMENTS
Approximately 36 cm (15 in) high

MATERIALS
- 1 x 50 g ball of Rowan 4 ply Cotton in Light Pink
- 1 x 50 g ball of Rowan 4 ply Soft in Red
- 1 x 50 g ball of Rowan 4 ply Soft in Pink
- 1 x 25 g ball of Rowan Kidsilk Haze in Fuchsia
- Oddments of 4 ply in Yellow, Black and Pink
- Pair each of 2¾ mm (UK12/US 2) and 3¼ mm (UK 10/US 3) knitting needles
- Washable toy stuffing
- Shirring elastic

ABBREVIATIONS
See page 14.

TENSION
4 ply Cotton
32 sts and 42 rows to 10 cm (4 in) measured over stocking stitch using 2¾mm (UK 12 /US 2) needles.
Kidsilk Haze
25 sts and 34 rows to 10 cm (4 in) measured over stocking stitch using 3¼mm (UK 10/US 3) needles.

DOLL
BACK
With 2¾ mm (UK 12/US 2) needles and Light Pink, cast on 43 sts.
Beg with a k row, work 44 rows in st st.
Mark each end of last row with a coloured thread.
Work a further 51 rows.
Next row: P20, cast off next 3 sts, p to end.
Cont in stripes of 2 rows Red and 2 rows Pink.
Cont on last set of sts for first leg.

Work 52 rows in st st.
Mark each end of last row. **
Work 6 rows.
Cont in Red only.
Shape Heel
Next row: K11, skpo, k1, turn.
Next row: P4, p2tog, p1, turn.
Next row: K5, skpo, k1, turn.
Next row: P6, p2tog, p1, turn.
Cont in this way, dec 1 st as set on every row until 12 sts rem, ending with a p row.
Break yarn and leave these sts on a holder.
Now cont in stripes of 2 rows Pink and 2 rows Red.
With RS facing and beg at marker, pick up and k 8 sts from side of heel, k12 sts from holder, pick up and k 8 sts from other side of heel to marker. (28 sts.)

Cont in st st, dec 1 st at each end of 4 foll 4th rows.
(20 sts.)
Work 7 rows.
Shape Toes
*** **Next row:** K1, skpo, k to last 3 sts, k2tog, k1.
P 1 row.
Rep last 2 rows once more. (16 sts.)
K 1 row.
Next 2 rows: P 11, turn, k to end.
Next 2 rows: P6, turn, k to end. ***
Break yarn and leave these sts on a spare needle.
With RS facing, rejoin yarn to rem sts for second leg
and work as given for first leg, reversing shaping.

FRONT
Work as given for Back to **.
Work a further 24 rows in st st.
Shape Toes
Work as given for Back from *** to ***.
With RS of back and front together and taking 1 st
from each needle and working them tog, cast off toe
sts.
With right side facing, rejoin yarn to rem sts for
second leg and complete as given for first leg,
reversing toe shaping.

ARMS (make 2)
With 2¾ mm (UK 12/US 2) needles and Light Pink,
cast on 30 sts.
Beg with a k row work 46 rows in st st.
Shape thumb
Next row: K15, m1, k15.
P 1 row.
Next row: K15, m1, k1, m1, k15.
P 1 row.
Next row: K15, m1, k3, m1, k15.
P 1 row.
Next row: K15, m1, k5, m1, k15.
P 1 row.
Next row: K22, turn and cast on 1 st.
Next row: P8, turn and cast on 1 st.
Work 4 rows on these 9 sts.
Next row: K1, [k2tog] 4 times.
Break yarn, thread end through rem sts, pull up,
secure, then join thumb seam.
With RS facing, rejoin yarn at base of thumb, pick up
and k2 sts from base of thumb, k to end.
(32 sts.) Work 9 rows.
Shape fingers
Next 2 rows: Work to last 4 sts, turn.
Next 2 rows: Work to last 8 sts, turn.

Next 2 rows: Work to last 12 sts, turn.
Next row: K4.
With RS together, fold arm in half, taking 1 st from
each needle and working them together, cast off.

TO MAKE UP
Join back and front together, leaving cast-on edge
free. Stuff firmly.
Wind a length of yarn twice round neck edge, pull up
tightly and secure.
Stuff head, gather cast-on edge, pull up and secure,
join gathers to form a seam across top of head. Work
a few lines of stitching in feet to form toes.
Join arm seams, leaving end open, stuff firmly and
close opening. Work a few lines of stitching in hands
to form fingers. Sew to side seams of body.

FACIAL FEATURES
Work in satin stitch for nose in Light Pink.
Work French knots using 6 wraps for eyes in Black.
Work stem stitch for mouth in Pink.

HAIR
Cut yellow yarn into 43-cm (17-in) lengths. Back-stitch
centre of lengths into position of the centre parting
on doll's head from just above neck at back to
forehead. Using Pink, make 2 twisted cords and
thread through side of head. Tie hair into position
and trim hair.

SKIRT

Using 2¾mm (UK 12/US 2) needles and Pink, cast on 60 sts.

Work 6 rows single rib.

Change to 3¼mm (UK 10/US 3) needles.

Cont in st st.

Work 2 rows.

Inc row: K8, m1, k to last 8 sts, m1, k8.

Work 3 rows.

Rep the last 4 rows 5 times more. (72 sts.)

K 4 rows.

Cast off.

TO MAKE UP

Join side seams. Thread shirring elastic through waist to fit doll.

JUMPER

BACK

With 2¾mm (UK 12/US 2) needles and Pink, cast on 56 sts.

Beg with a k row, work 6 rows in st st.

Change to 3¼mm (UK 10/US 3) needles and Fuchsia.

Work 34 rows in st st.

Shape neck

Next row: K16, turn, and work on these sts for first side of neck.

Dec 1 st at neck edge on next 3 rows. (13 sts.)

Cast off.

With RS of work facing slip centre 24 sts on a holder.

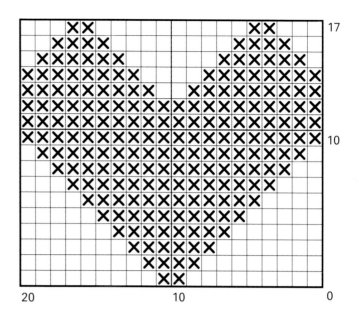

☐ Fuchsia

☒ Pink

Rejoin yarn to next st, k to end.

Complete to match first side of neck shaping.

FRONT

Work as given for back until 12 rows have been worked in Fuchsia.

Place motif

Next row: K18, work across row 1 of Chart, k18.

Using the intarsia method, cont to end of Chart.

Work a further 3 rows.

Shape neck

Next row: K18, turn, and work on these sts for first side of neck.

Dec 1 st at neck edge on next 5 rows. (13 sts.)

Cast off.

With right side of work facing slip centre 20 sts on a holder.

Rejoin yarn to next st, k to end.

Complete to match first side of neck shaping.

Neckband

Join right shoulder seam.

With right side facing, using 2¾ mm (UK 12/US 2) needles and Pink, pick up and k6 sts down left side of front neck, k across 20 sts at centre front, pick up and k 6 sts up right side of front neck, 4 sts down right side of back neck, k across 24 sts at centre back neck, pick up and k 4 sts up left side of back neck. (64 sts.)

Beg with a p row, work 5 rows in st st.

Cast off.

SLEEVES

With 2¾ mm (UK 12/US 2) needles and Pink cast on 38 sts.

Work 6 rows in st st.

Change to 3¼ mm (UK 10/US 3) needles and Fuchsia. Inc and work into st st 1 st at each end of the 3rd and 3 foll 4th rows. (46 sts.)

Work straight to 11 cm (4½ in), ending with a p row. Cast off.

Join left shoulder and neckband seam. Sew on sleeves. Join side and sleeve seams.

GIRL'S SHOES

With 3¼ mm (UK10/US 3) needles and Red, cast on 48 sts.

K1 row.

1st row: K1, yfwd, k22, yfwd, k2, yfwd, k22, yfwd, k1.

2nd and 4th rows: K to end, working k1 tbl into yfwd of previous row.

3rd row: K2, yfwd, k23, yfwd, k2, yfwd, k23, yfwd, k2.

5th row: K3, yfwd, k24, yfwd, k2, yfwd, k24, yfwd, k3. (60 sts.)

6th row: K to end, working k1 tbl into yfwd of previous row.

K10 rows.

Shape top

Next row: K27, k2tog, k2, skpo, k27.

K1 row.

Next row: K26, k2tog, k2, skpo, k26.

K1 row.

Next row: K25, k2tog, k2, skpo, k25.

K1 row.

Cast off rem 54 sts.

Join back and sole seam. Make 2 twisted cords and thread through cast-off edge to tie at centre front.

Boy rag doll

Why limit yourself to just a girl rag doll when you can knit a boy rag doll too? You can make a whole wardrobe of clothes and let your child play dressing up with her or his doll.

SKILL LEVEL 3

MEASUREMENTS
Approximately 36 cm (14 in) high

MATERIALS
• 2 x 50 g balls of Rowan 4 ply Cotton in Pale Pink
• 1 x 50 g ball of Rowan 4 ply Soft in each of Grey and Turquoise
• 1 x 25 g ball of Rowan Kidsilk Haze in Light Grey
• Oddments of DK Brown for hair, 4 ply Black for eyes and Pink for mouth and nose
• Pair each of 2¾ mm (UK 12/US 2), 3 mm (UK 11/US 2/3) and 3¼ mm (UK 10/US 3) knitting needles
• Washable toy stuffing
• Shirring elastic

ABBREVIATIONS
See page 14.

TENSION
4 ply Cotton
32 sts and 42 rows to 10 cm (4 in) measured over stocking stitch using 2¾ mm (UK 12 /US 2) needles.
Kidsilk Haze
25 sts and 34 rows to 10 cm (4 in) measured over stocking stitch using 3¼ mm (UK 10/US 3) needles.

DOLL
BACK
With 2¾ mm (UK 12/US 2) needles and Pale Pink, cast on 43 sts.
Beg with a k row, work 44 rows in st st.
Mark each end of last row with a coloured thread.
Cont in st st for a further 51 rows.
Next row: P20, cast off next 3 sts, p to end.
Cont on last set of sts for first leg.
Work 52 rows in st st.
Mark each end of last row. **
Work 6 rows.
Shape Heel
Next row: K11, skpo, k1, turn.
Next row: P4, p2tog, p1, turn.
Next row: K5, skpo, k1, turn.
Next row: P6, p2tog, p1, turn.
Cont in this way, dec 1 st as set on every row until 12 sts rem, ending with a p row.
Break yarn and leave these sts on a holder.
With RS facing and beg at marker, pick up and k 8 sts from side of heel, k12 sts from holder, pick up and k 8 sts from other side of heel to marker. (28 sts.)
Cont in st st, dec 1 st at each end of 4 foll 4th rows. (20 sts.)
Work 7 rows.
Shape Toes
*** **Next row:** K1, skpo, k to last 3 sts, k2tog, k1.
P 1 row.
Rep last 2 rows once more. (16 sts.)
K 1 row.
Next 2 rows: P 11, turn, k to end.
Next 2 rows: P6, turn, k to end. ***
Break yarn and leave these sts on a spare needle.
With RS facing, rejoin yarn to rem sts for second leg and work as given for first leg, reversing shaping.

FRONT

Work as given for Back to **.

Work a further 24 rows in st st.

Shape Toes

Work as given for Back from *** to ***.

With RS of back and front together and taking 1 st from each needle and working them tog, cast off toe sts.

With RS facing, rejoin yarn to rem sts for second leg and complete as given for first leg, reversing toe shaping.

ARMS (make 2)

With 2¾ mm (UK 12/US 2) needles and Pale Pink, cast on 30 sts.

Beg with a k row work 46 rows in st st.

Shape thumb

Next row: K15, m1, k15.

P 1 row.

Next row: K15, m1, k1, m1, k15.

P 1 row.

Next row: K15, m1, k3, m1, k15.

P 1 row.

Next row: K15, m1, k5, m1, k15.

P 1 row.

Next row: K22, turn and cast on 1 st.

Next row: P8, turn and cast on 1 st.

Work 4 rows on these 9 sts.

Next row: K1, [k2tog] 4 times.

Break off yarn, thread end through rem sts, pull up, secure, then join thumb seam.

With RS facing, rejoin yarn at base of thumb, pick up and k 2 sts from base of thumb, k to end. (32 sts.) Work 9 rows.

Shape fingers

Next 2 rows: Work to last 4 sts, turn.

Next 2 rows: Work to last 8 sts, turn.

Next 2 rows: Work to last 12 sts, turn.

Next row: K4.

With RS together, fold arm in half, taking 1 st from each needle and working them together, cast off.

TO MAKE UP

Join back and front together, leaving cast-on edge free. Stuff firmly. Wind a length of yarn twice round neck edge, pull up tightly and secure. Stuff head, gather cast-on edge, pull up and secure, join gathers to form a seam across top of head. Work a few lines of stitching in feet to form toes. Join arm seams, leaving end open, stuff firmly and close opening.

Work a few lines of stitching in hands to form fingers. Sew to side seams of body.

FACIAL FEATURES

Work in satin stitch for nose in Pale Pink.

Work French knots using 6 wraps for eyes in Black.

Work stem stitch for mouth in pink.

HAIR

Make a fringe by sewing loops of brown yarn at top of head to front of forehead. Cut loops to form a fringe. Cut brown yarn into 20-cm (8-in) lengths. Back stitch the centre of lengths into position of the centre parting on doll's head from just above neck at back to forehead. Trim hair.

TROUSERS

Using 2¾ mm (UK 12/US 2) needles and Turquoise, cast on 60 sts.

Work 6 rows single rib.

Change to 3¼ mm (UK 10/US 3) needles.

Cont in st st until leg measures 8½ cm (3¼ in) from cast-on edge.

Shape crotch

Cast off 3 sts at beg of next 2 rows. (54 sts.)

Inc 1 st at each end of the next and every foll 6th row until there are 60 sts.

Work 2 rows.

K4 rows.

Cast off.

TO MAKE UP

Join inner leg seams. Join front and back seam.

Thread shirring elastic through waist to fit doll.

JUMPER

BACK

With 2¾ mm (UK 12/US 2) needles and Turquoise, cast on 57 sts.

Beg with a k row, work 6 rows in st st.

Change to 3¼ mm (UK 10/US 3) needles and Light Grey.

Work 34 rows in st st.

Shape neck

Next row: K16, turn, and work on these sts for first side of neck.

Dec 1 st at neck edge on next 3 rows. (13 sts.)

Cast off.

With RS of work facing slip centre 25 sts on a holder.

Rejoin yarn to next st, k to end.

Complete to match first side of neck shaping.

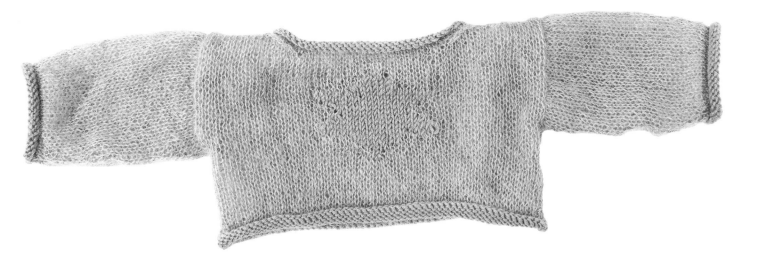

FRONT

Work as given for back until 12 rows have been worked in light grey.

Place motif

Next row: K19, work across row 1 of Chart, k19. Using the intarsia method, cont to end of Chart. Work a further 3 rows.

Shape neck

Next row: K18, turn, and work on these sts for first side of neck.

Dec 1 st at neck edge on next 5 rows. (13 sts.) Cast off.

With RS of work facing slip centre 21 sts on a holder. Rejoin yarn to next st, k to end.

Complete to match first side of neck shaping.

Neckband

Join right shoulder seam.

With RS facing, using 2¾ mm (UK 12/US 2) needles and Turquoise, pick up and k6 sts down left side of front neck, k across 21 sts at centre front, pick up and k 6 sts up right side of front neck, 4 sts down right side of back neck, k across 25 sts at centre back neck, pick up and k 4 sts up left side of back neck. (66 sts.)

Beg with a p row, work 5 rows in st st. Cast off.

SLEEVES

With 2¾ mm (UK 12/US 2) needles and Turquoise, cast on 38 sts.

Work 6 rows in st st.

Change to 3¼ mm (UK 10/US 3) needles and Light Grey.

Inc and work in st st 1 st at each end of the 3rd and 3 foll 4th rows. (46 sts.)

Work straight to 11 cm (4½ in), ending with a p row. Cast off.

MAKE UP

Join left shoulder and neckband seam. Sew on sleeves. Join side and sleeve seams.

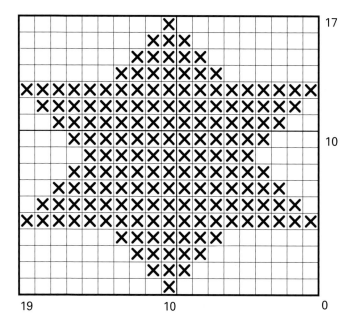

☐ Light Grey
☒ Turquoise

SOCKS

With 3 ¼ mm (UK 10/US 3) needles and Turquoise, cast on 36 sts.

Rib row: * K1, p1; rep from * to end.

Rib a further 9 rows.

Change to 3 mm (UK 11/US 2/3) needles.

Work 10 rows rib, dec 4 sts on last row. (32 sts.)

Change to 3¼ mm (UK 10/US 3) needles.

Beg with a k row, cont in st st.

Work 5 rows.

Shape heel

Next row: P9 sts only, turn.

Work 9 rows in st st on these 9 sts only.

Dec row: P3, p2tog, p1, turn.

Next row: Sl 1, k4.

Dec row: P4, p2tog, p1, turn.

Next row: Sl 1, k5.

Dec row: P5, p2tog.

Break yarn and leave rem 6 sts on a holder.

With WS facing, slip centre 14 sts on to a holder, rejoin yarn to rem 9 sts, p to end.

Work 8 rows in st st on these 9 sts.

Dec row: K3, k2tog tbl, k1, turn.

Next row: Sl 1, p4.

Dec row: K4, k2tog tbl, k1, turn.

Next row: Sl 1, p5.

Dec row: K4, k2tog tbl, k1, turn.

Next row: Sl 1, p5.

Shape instep

Next row: K6, pick up and k 8 sts evenly along inside edge of heel, k 14 sts from holder, pick up and k 8 sts along inside edge of heel and k 6 sts from holder. (42 sts.)

P 1 row.

Dec row: K12, k2tog, k14, k2tog tbl, k12.

P 1 row.

Dec row: K11, k2tog, k14, k2tog tbl, k11.

P 1 row.

Dec row: K10, k2tog, k14, k2tog tbl, k10.

P 1 row.

Dec row: K9, k2tog, k14, k2tog tbl, k9. (34 sts.)

Work 17 rows straight.

Shape toes

Dec row: K6, k2tog, k2, skpo, k10, k2tog, k2, skpo, k6.

P 1 row.

Dec row: K5, k2tog, k2, skpo, k8, k2tog, k2, skpo, k5.

P 1 row.

Dec row: K4, k2tog, k2, skpo, k6, k2tog, k2, skpo, k4.

P 1 row.

Dec row: K3, k2tog, k2, skpo, k4, k2tog, k2, skpo, k3.

P 1 row. Cast off rem sts.

Join back of foot seam.

SHOES

With 3¼ mm (UK 10/US 3) needles and Grey, cast on 48 sts.

K 1 row.

1st row: K1, yfwd, k22, yfwd, k2, yfwd, k22, yfwd, k1.

2nd and 4th rows: K to end, working k1 tbl into yfwd of previous row.

3rd row: K2, yfwd, k23, yfwd, k2, yfwd, k23, yfwd, k2.

5th row: K3, yfwd, k24, yfwd, k2, yfwd, k24, yfwd, k3. (60 sts.)

6th row: K to end, working k1 tbl into yfwd of previous row.

K 10 rows.

Shape top

Next row: K27, k2tog, k2, skpo, k27.

K 1 row.

Next row: K26, k2tog, k2, skpo, k26.

K 1 row.

Next row: K25, k2tog, k2, skpo, k25.

K 1 row.

Next row: K24, k2tog, k2, skpo, k24.

K 1 row.

Next row: K23, k2tog, k2, skpo, k23.

K 1 row.

Next row: K22, k2tog, k2, skpo, k22.

K 1 row.

Cast off rem 48 sts.

Join back and sole seam. Make two 30-cm (12-in) long twisted cords and thread through cast-off edge to tie at centre front.

Panda

The endangered Giant Panda is one of the most popular animals in the world. This gorgeous knitted toy will appeal to children of all ages.

SKILL LEVEL 3

MEASUREMENTS
33 cm (13 in) high

MATERIALS
- 3 x 50 g balls of Jaeger Matchmaker Merino DK in Black
- 2 x 50 g balls of Jaeger Matchmaker Merino DK in White
- Pair of 4½ mm (UK 7/US 7) knitting needles
- Washable toy stuffing
Use two strands of yarn together throughout.

ABBREVIATIONS
See page 14.

TENSION
19 stitches and 27 rows to 10 cm (4 in) measured over stocking stitch using 4½ mm (UK 7/US 7) needles.

BODY FRONT (make 1)
Crotch gusset: With 4½ mm (UK 7/US 7) needles and White, cast on 3 sts. Mark centre st. Beg with a k row, cont in st st, work 1 row. Inc 1 st at each end of next 8 rows and 2 foll alt rows. (23 sts.) P 1 row. Mark each end of last row.
Shape legholes: Cast off 2 sts at beg of next 2 rows. Dec 1 st at each end of next row and foll alt row, then on 2 foll 3rd rows. (11 sts.) St st 5 rows. Inc 1 st at each end of next 10 rows, thus completing leghole shaping. (31 sts.)
St st 10 rows.
Using separate small balls of yarn for each coloured area and twisting yarns together on wrong side at join, cont thus:
1st row: K2 Black, 27 White, 2 Black.
2nd row: P5 Black, 21 White, 5 Black.

3rd row: K8 Black, 15 White, 8 Black.
4th row: P11 Black, 9 White, 11 Black.
5th row: K13 Black, 5 White, 13 Black.
Cont in Black only, p 1 row.
Shape armholes: Cast off 2 sts at beg of next 2 rows. Dec 1 st at each end of next row and 3 foll alt rows. (19 sts.)
Shape neck: Next row: P5, cast off next 9 sts, p to end. **Next row:** K2tog, k1, k2tog, turn.
Next row: P2tog, p1. K2tog and fasten off.
Rejoin yarn at inside edge to rem 5 sts, k2tog, k1, k2tog.
Next row: P1, p2tog. K2tog and fasten off.

BODY BACK (make 1)
First side: With 4½ mm (UK 7/US 7) needles and White, cast on 3 sts. Beg with a k row, cont in st st, work 1 row. Mark end of last row. P 1 row. Cast on 3 sts at beg of next row and 2 foll alt rows. (12 sts.) P 1 row. Leave these sts.
Second side: With 4½ mm (UK 7/US 7) needles and White, cast on 3 sts. Beg with a k row, cont in st st, work 1 row. Mark beg of last row. Cast on 3 sts at beg of next row and 3 foll alt rows. (15 sts.) Mark 2nd sts from beg of last row.
Joining row: K15 sts from second side then 12 sts from first side. (27 sts.)
St st 9 rows. Inc 1 st at each end of next 8 rows, thus completing leghole shaping. (43 sts.) St st 10 rows. Cont thus:
1st row: K2 Black, 39 White, 2 Black.
2nd row: P4 Black, 35 White, 4 Black.
3rd row: K6 Black, 31 White, 6 Black.
4th row: P7 Black, 29 White, 7 Black.
5th row: K8 Black, 27 White, 8 Black.
6th row: P9 Black, 25 White, 9 Black.
Shape armholes: 7th row: With Black, cast off 2 sts, k 7 sts more, 23 White, 10 Black.
8th row: With Black, cast off 2 sts, p 8 sts more, 21 White, 9 Black.

9th row: With Black, k2tog, k8, 19 White, with Black, k8, k2tog.

10th row: P11 Black, 15 White, 11 Black.

11th row: With Black, k2tog, k11, 11 White, with Black, k11, k2tog.

12th row: P14 Black, 7 White, 14 Black.

Cont in Black only, dec 1 st at each end of next row and 3 foll alt rows. (27 sts.)

Shape neck: Next row: P8, cast off next 11 sts, p to end.

Next row: K2tog, k6, turn. Cast off 3 sts at beg of next row. (4 sts.) Cast off rem sts.

Rejoin yarn at inside edge to rem 8 sts, cast off 3 sts, k2 more sts, k2tog. (4 sts.) P 1 row. Cast off rem sts.

RIGHT LEG (make 1)

With 4½ mm (UK 7/US 7) needles and Black, cast on 41 sts. Beginning with a k row, st st 6 rows.

Shape instep: Next row: K24, [k2tog, k1] twice, k2tog, k9.

Next row: P8, cast off next 7sts, p to end.

Next row: Inc, k21, k2tog, k6, inc. (32 sts.)

Inc 1 st at each end of 2 foll 4th rows. (36 sts.)

St st 3 rows.

Shape top: Cast off 4 sts at beg of next 2 rows.

Dec 1 st at each end of next row and 2 foll alt rows, then on next 3 rows. Cast off 3 sts at beg of next 2 rows. (10 sts.) Cast off.

LEFT LEG (make 1)

Work as given for left leg, reversing shapings, by reading p for k and k for p.

SOLES (make 2)

With 4½ mm (UK 7/US 7) needles and Black, cast on 5 sts. K 1 row. Cont in st st, inc 1 st at each end of next 2 rows and 2 foll alt rows. (13 sts.) St st 7 rows. Dec 1 st at each end of next row and 2 foll alt rows. Dec 1 st at each end of next row. (5 sts.) Cast off.

RIGHT ARM (make 1)

With 4½ mm (UK 7/US 7) needles and Black, cast on 13 sts. Beg with a k row, st st 2 rows.

1st inc row: Inc, k4, inc, k1, inc, k4, inc. (17 sts.) P 1 row.

2nd inc row: K2, inc, [k3, inc] 3 times, k2. (21 sts.) P 1 row.

3rd inc row: K2, inc, [k4, inc] 3 times, k3. (25 sts.) P 1 row.

4th inc row: K3, inc, [k5, inc] 3 times, k3. (29 sts.) St st 7 rows. **

Shape elbow: 1st row: K26, yfwd, sl 1, yb, turn.

2nd row: Sl 1, p11, yb, sl 1, yfwd, turn.

3rd row: Sl 1, k8, yfwd, sl 1, yb, turn.

4th row: Sl 1, p5, yb, sl 1, yfwd, turn.

5th row: Sl 1, k7, yfwd, sl 1, yb, turn.

6th row: Sl 1, p9, yb, sl 1, yfwd, turn.

7th row: Sl 1, k11, yfwd, sl 1, yb, turn.

8th row: Sl 1, p13, yb, sl 1, yfwd, turn.

9th row: Sl 1, k15.

St st 5 rows across all sts.

Shape top: Cast off 2 sts at beginning of next 2 rows. Dec 1 st at each end of next row and 4 foll alt rows. (15 sts.) P 1 row.

Next row: Cast off 4 sts, k to last 2 sts, dec. Rep last 2 rows, once more. (5 sts.) Cast off.

LEFT ARM (make 1)

Work as right arm to **.

Shape elbow: 1st row: K14, yfwd, sl 1, yb, turn.

2nd row: Sl 1, p11, yb, sl 1, yfwd, turn.

3rd row: Sl 1, k8, yfwd, sl 1, yb, turn.

4th row: Sl 1, p5, yb, sl 1, yfwd, turn.

5th row: Sl 1, k7, yfwd, sl 1, yb, turn.

6th row: Sl 1, p9, yb, sl 1, yfwd, turn.

7th row: Sl 1, k11, yfwd, sl 1, yb, turn.

8th row: Sl 1, p13, yb, sl 1, yfwd, turn.

9th row: Sl 1, k27.

St st 5 rows across all sts.

Shape top: Cast off 2 sts at beginning of next 2 rows. Dec 1 st at each end of next row and 4 foll alt rows. (15 sts.) P 1 row. Dec 1 st at beg of next row. Cast off 4 sts at beg of next row. Rep last 2 rows, once more. (5 sts.) Cast off.

HEAD

With 4½ mm (UK 7/US 7) needles and White, cast on 14 sts. Beg with a k row, st st 2 rows.

Shape back head: Cast on 4 sts at beg of next 8 rows. (46 sts.) K 1 row.

1st row: P43, yb, sl 1, yfwd, turn.

2nd row: Sl 1, k40, yfwd, sl 1, yb, turn.

3rd row: Sl 1, p38, yb, sl 1, yfwd, turn.

4th row: Sl 1, k36, yfwd, sl 1, yb, turn.

5th row: Sl 1, p34, yb, sl 1, yfwd, turn.

6th row: Sl 1, k32, yfwd, sl 1, yb, turn.

7th row: Sl 1, p30, yb, sl 1, yfwd, turn.

8th row: Sl 1, k28, yfwd, sl 1, yb, turn.

9th row: Sl 1, p25, yb, sl 1, yfwd, turn.

10th row: Sl 1, k22, yfwd, sl 1, yb, turn.

11th row: Sl 1, p19, yb, sl 1, yfwd, turn.

12th row: Sl 1, k16, yfwd, sl 1, yb, turn.

13th row: Sl 1, p13, yb, sl 1, yfwd, turn.
14th row: Sl 1, k10, yfwd, sl 1, yb, turn.
15th row: Sl 1, p7, yb, sl 1, yfwd, turn.
16th row: Sl 1, k4, yfwd, sl 1, yb, turn.
Next row: Sl 1, p to end.
Inc row: Cast on 3 sts, k these 3 sts, k5, inc, [k4, inc] 7 times, k5, turn and cast on 3 sts. (60 sts.) P 1 row.
Shape top head: 1st row: Cast on 4 sts, k these 4 sts, k35, yfwd, sl 1, yb, turn.
2nd row: Sl 1, p10, yb, sl 1, yfwd, turn.
3rd row: Sl 1, k14, yfwd, sl 1, yb, turn.
4th row: Sl 1, p18, yb, sl 1, yfwd, turn.
5th row: Sl 1, k22, yfwd, sl 1, yb, turn.
6th row: Sl 1, p26, yb, sl 1, yfwd, turn.
7th row: Sl 1, k30, yfwd, sl 1, yb, turn.
8th row: Sl 1, p34, yb, sl 1, yfwd, turn.
9th row: Sl 1, k38, yfwd, sl 1, yb, turn.
10th row: Sl 1, p42, yb, sl 1, yfwd, turn.
11th row: Sl 1, k37, yfwd, sl 1, yb, turn.
12th row: Sl 1, p32, yb, sl 1, yfwd, turn.
13th row: Sl 1, k27, yfwd, sl 1, yb, turn.
14th row: Sl 1, p22, yb, sl 1, yfwd, turn.
15th row: Sl 1, k19, yfwd, sl 1, yb, turn.
16th row: Sl 1, p16, yb, sl 1, yfwd, turn.
17th row: Sl 1, k33, yfwd, sl 1, yb, turn.
18th row: Sl 1, p50, yb, sl 1, yfwd, turn.
Shape face: 1st dec row: Sl 1, k1, k2tog, [k5, k2tog] 7 times, k4, turn and cast on 4 sts. (60 sts.) Mark each end of last row. St st 3 rows.
2nd dec row: K8, k2tog, [k4, k2tog] 7 times, k8. (52 sts.) P 1 row.
3rd dec row: K4, k2tog, [k4, k2tog] 7 times, k4. (44 sts.) P 1 row.
4th dec row: [K3, k2tog] 8 times, k4. (36 sts.) P 1 row. Cast off tightly.

Shape snout With RS facing, pick up and k 36 sts along cast off row. Beg with a p row, st st 3 rows.
1st dec row: [K4, k2tog] 6 times. (30 sts.) St st 3 rows.
2nd dec row: [K2tog, k3] 6 times. (24 sts.) P 1 row.
3rd dec row: [K1, k2tog] 8 times. (16 sts.)
4th dec row: [P2tog] 8 times. (8 sts.) Break off yarn, leaving a long end. Thread end through rem sts, pull up and secure.

EARS (make 4)
With 4½ mm (UK 7/US 7) needles and Black, cast on 13 sts. St st 4 rows. Dec 1 st at each end of next row and 2 foll alt rows. (7 sts.) Dec 1 st at each end of next row. (5 sts.) Cast off.

NOSE (make 1)
With 4½ mm (UK 7/US 7) needles and Black, cast on 5 sts. St st 3 rows. Dec 1 st at each end of next row. Work 3tog and fasten off.

EYES PATCHES
With 4½ mm (UK 7/US 7) needles and Black, cast on 5 sts. K 1 row. Cont in st st, inc 1 st at each end of next 2 rows. (9 sts.) St st 7 rows.
Next row: Dec, k to end.
Next row: P to last 2 sts, dec. Dec 1 st at each end of next 2 rows. (3 sts.) Cast off. Make one more, reversing shapings by reading p for k and k for p.

TO MAKE UP
Join sides of body pieces together from top of leghole to beginning of armhole shaping. Sew in front crotch gusset to lower edge of back, matching markers.
Join leg seams, with this seam running at centre of inside of each leg, join together cast-off sts of instep. Sew in soles.
Join row ends of arms, then with this seam running at centre of inside of each arm, join together cast-on edge. Sew legs and arms in place. Stuff legs, body and arms firmly.
Join head seam from marker to top of snout. Stuff head firmly. With the end of head seam at centre of front neck of body, stitch head in place. Join paired ear pieces together, position on head and sew in place.
Sew on nose piece, then with Black, embroider mouth. Position eye patches on head and stitch in place. Using White, embroider circle of 7 chain stitches on each patch for eyes.

Rabbits

Worked in a fluffy tweed yarn, these cuddly rabbits will delight any child. Knit practical dungarees or a pretty little dress for a day's outing, then later snuggle down and go to sleep with these loveable rabbits. Sweet dreams.

SKILL LEVEL 3

MEASUREMENTS
Large rabbit is approximately 39 cm (15½ in tall)
Small rabbit is approximately 20 cm (8 in) tall

MATERIALS
• 3 x 50 g balls of Rowan Kid Classic in Grey
• Oddments of Rowan Kid Classic in Pale Pink and Pale Blue
• 1 x 50 g ball of Jaeger Baby Merino DK in Blue
• 1 x 50 g ball of Jaeger Baby Merino DK in Pink
• Oddments of black and pale pink embroidery thread
• Pair each of 3¼ mm (UK 10/US 3), 3¾ mm (UK 9/US 5) and 4 mm (UK 8/US 6) knitting needles
• 3 small buttons

ABBREVIATIONS
See page 14.

TENSION
20 sts and 27 rows to 10 cm (4 in) measured over stocking stitch using 3¾ mm (UK 9/US 5) needles.

LARGE RABBIT
LEGS (make 2)
With 3¾ mm (UK 9/US 5) needles and Grey, cast on 24 sts.
P 1 row.
Next row: K1, [m1, k1] to end. (47 sts.)
P 1 row.
Next row: K1, m1, k20, [m1, k1] 6 times, k19, m1, k1. (55 sts.)
Work 7 rows.
Next row: K25, k2tog, k1, skpo, k25.

P 1 row.
Next row: K24, k2tog, k1, skpo, k24.
P 1 row.
Next row: K23, k2tog, k1, skpo, k23.
P 1 row.
Next row: K22, k2tog, k1, skpo, k22. (47 sts.)
P 1 row.
Next row: K13, cast off next 21 sts, k to end.
Work 17 rows in st st across all 26 sts.
Next row: K3, k2tog, k3, skpo, k5, k2tog, k3, skpo, k4.
P 1 row.
Next row: K2, k2tog, k3, skpo, k3, k2tog, k3, skpo, k3. (18 sts.)
P 1 row. Cast off.

BODY
Begin at neck edge.
With 3¾ mm (UK 9/US 5) needles and Grey, cast on 33 sts.
P 1 row.
Next row: k1, [m1, k1] to end. (65 sts.)
Beg with a p row, work 5 rows in st st.
Next row: [K8, m1] 4 times, k1, [m1, k8] 4 times. (73 sts.)
Work 3 rows.
Next row: K36, m1, k1, m1, k36. (75 sts.)
Work 35 rows.
Next row: K35, skpo, k1, k2tog, k35.
Work 3 rows.
Next row: K34, skpo, k1, k2tog, k34.
Work 3 rows.
Next row: K33, skpo, k1, k2tog, k33.
Work 3 rows.
Next row: K32, skpo, k1, k2tog, k32.
Work 3 rows.
Next row: K31, skpo, k1, k2tog, k31. (65 sts.)
P 1 row.
Cast off.

ARMS (make 2)

With 3¾ mm (UK 9/US 5) needles and Grey, cast on 6 sts.

P 1 row.

Next row: K1, [m1, k1] to end. (11 sts.)

Rep last 2 rows once more. (21 sts.)

P 1 row.

Next row: K1, [m1, k4, m1, k1] 4 times. (29 sts.)

P 1 row.

Next row: K1, [m1, k6, m1, k1] 4 times. (37 sts.)

Work 15 rows.

Next row: K1, [skpo, k13, k2tog, k1] twice. (33 sts.)

Work 3 rows.

Inc 1 st at each end of next row. (35 sts.)

Work 19 rows.

Next row: K1, [skpo, k12, k2tog, k1] twice. (31 sts.)

P 1 row.

Next row: K1, [skpo, k10, k2tog, k1] twice. (27 sts.)

P 1 row.

Next row: K1, [k2tog] to end. (14 sts.)

P 1 row.

Next row: [K2tog] to end. (7 sts.)

Break yarn, thread through rem sts, pull up tightly and fasten off securely.

Join underarm seam, leaving an opening.

Stuff firmly and close opening.

HEAD

With 3¾ mm (UK 9/US 5) needles and Grey, cast on 7 sts.

P 1 row.

Next row: K1, [m1, k1] to end.

Rep the last 2 rows twice more. (49 sts.)

Work 3 rows in st st.

Next row: K1, [m1, k3] to end. (65 sts.)

Work 3 rows.

Next row: K1, [m1, k4] to end. (81 sts.)

Work 5 rows.

Next row: K1, skpo, k35, k2tog, k1, skpo, k35, k2tog, k1.

P 1 row.

Next row: K1, skpo, k33, k2tog, k1, skpo, k33, k2tog, k1.

P 1 row.

Next row: K1, skpo, k31, k2tog, k1, skpo, k31, k2tog, k1. (69 sts.)

P 1 row.

Next row: K1, skpo, k29, k2tog, k1, skpo, k29, k2tog, k1.

P 1 row.

Next row: K1, skpo, k27, k2tog, k1, skpo, k27, k2tog, k1.

P 1 row.

Next row: K1, skpo, k25, k2tog, k1, skpo, k25, k2tog, k1. (57 sts.)

P 1 row.

Next row: K1, [skpo] 6 times, k1, [k2tog] 7 times, k1, [skpo] 7 times, k1, [k2tog] 6 times, k1. (31 sts.)

P 1 row.

Next row: K1, [skpo] 3 times, k2, [k2tog] 3 times, k1, [skpo] 3 times, k2, [k2tog] 3 times, k1. (19 sts.)

P 1 row.

Next row: K1, [skpo] twice, [k2tog] twice, k1, [skpo] twice, [k2tog] twice, k1. (11 sts.)

P 1 row.

Next row: K1, skpo, k2tog, k1, skpo, k2tog, k1. (7 sts.)

P 1 row.

Break yarn, thread through rem sts, pull up tightly and fasten off securely.

EARS (make 2)
Outer Ears
With 3¾ mm (UK 9/US 5) needles and Grey, cast on 20 sts.

Work 26 rows st st.

Dec 1 st at each end of next and every foll alt row until 2 sts rem.

Work 2 tog and fasten off.

Inner Ears
With 3¾ mm (UK 9/US 5) needles and Pale Pink, cast on 18 sts.

Work 26 rows in st st.

Dec 1 st at each end of next and every foll alt row until 2 sts rem.

Work 2 tog and fasten off. Join ears into pairs.

TO MAKE UP
Fold sides of body to centre, join cast-off edge. Gather neck edge of body, pull up and secure. Join back seam, leaving an opening. Stuff firmly and close opening. Sew head in position. Sew ears in place. Attach arms and legs. Embroider French knots for eyes and stem stitch for mouth using Black. Embroider nose in satin stitch using Pink.

SMALL RABBIT
LEGS (make 2)
With 3¾ mm (UK 9/US 5) needles and Grey, cast on 12 sts.

P 1 row.

Next row: K1, [m1, k1] to end. (23 sts.)

P 1 row.

Next row: K1, m1, k8, [m1, k1] 6 times, k7, m1, k1. (31 sts.)

Work 3 rows.

Next row: K13, k2tog, k1, skpo, k13.

P 1 row.

Next row: K12, k2tog, k1, skpo, k12. (27 sts.)

P 1 row.

Next row: K7, cast off next 13 sts, k to end.

Work 7 rows in st st across all 14 sts.

Next row: K1, k2tog, k1, skpo, k2, k2tog, k1, skpo, k1. (10 sts.)

P 1 row.

Cast off.

BODY
Begin at neck edge.

With 3¾ mm (UK 9/US 5) needles and Grey, cast on 15 sts.

P 1 row.

Next row: K1, [m1, k1] to end. (29 sts.)

Beg with a p row work 5 rows in st st.

Next row: [K7, m1] twice, k1, [m1, k7] twice. (33 sts.)

Work 3 rows.

Next row: K16, m1, k1, m1, k16.

Work 17 rows.

Next row: K15, skpo, k1, k2tog, k15.

Work 3 rows.

Next row: K14, skpo, k1, k2tog, k14. (31 sts.)

P 1 row.

Cast off.

ARMS (make 2)
With 3¾ mm (UK 9/US 5) needles and Grey, cast on 6 sts.

P 1 row.

Next row: K1, [m1, k1] to end. (11 sts.)

P 1 row.

Next row: K1, [m1, k4, m1, k1] twice. (15 sts.)

Work 7 rows.

Next row: K1, [skpo, k2, k2tog, k1] twice. (11 sts.)

Work 3 rows.

Inc one st at each end of next row. (13 sts.)

Work 5 rows.

Next row: K1, [skpo, k1, k2tog, k1] twice. (9 sts.)

P 1 row.

Next row: K1, [k2tog] to end. (5 sts.)
Break yarn, thread through rem sts, pull up and fasten off securely.
Join underarm seam, leaving an opening.
Stuff firmly and close opening.

HEAD
With 3¾ mm (UK 9/US 5) needles and Grey, cast on 7 sts.
P 1 row.
Next row: K1, [m1, k1] to end.
Rep the last 2 rows once more. (25 sts.)
Work 3 rows in st st.
Next row: K1, [m1, k3] to end. (33 sts.)
Work 3 rows.
Next row: K1, [m1, k4] to end. (41 sts.)
P 1 row.
Next row: K1, skpo, k15, k2tog, k1, skpo, k15, k2tog, k1.
P 1 row.
Next row: K1, skpo, k13, k2tog, k1, skpo, k13, k2tog, k1.
P 1 row.

Next row: K1, skpo, k11, k2tog, k1, skpo, k11, k2tog, k1. (29 sts.)
P 1 row.
Next row: K1, [skpo] 3 times, k1, [k2tog] 3 times, k1, [skpo] 3 times, k1, [k2tog] 3 times, k1. (17 sts.)
P 1 row.
Next row: K1, skpo, sl 1, k2tog, psso, k2tog, k1, skpo, sl 1, k2tog, psso, k2tog, k1. (11 sts.)
P 1 row.
Break yarn, thread through rem sts, pull up and fasten off securely.

EARS (make 2)
Outer Ears
With 3¾ mm (UK 9/US 5) needles and Grey, cast on 14 sts.
Work 20 rows in st st.
Dec 1 st at each end of next and every foll alt row until 2 sts rem.
Work 2 tog and fasten off.
Inner Ears
With 3¾ mm (UK 9/US 5) needles and Pale Blue, cast on 12 sts.
Work 20 rows in st st.
Dec 1 st at each end of next and every foll alt row until 2 sts rem.
Work 2 tog and fasten off. Join ears together in pairs.

TO MAKE UP
Work as for Large Rabbit, noting that purl side of work is RS.

DRESS
FRONT
With 3¾ mm (UK 10/US 3) needles and Pink, cast on 42 sts.
K 3 rows.
Change 4 mm (UK 8/US 6) needles.
Cont in st st.
Work 16 rows.
Dec row: K1, *k2tog; rep from * to last st, k1. (22 sts.)
Change to 3¾ mm (UK 10/US 3) needles.
K 3 rows.
Change to 4 mm (UK 8/US 6) needles. **
St st 4 rows.
Next row: K to end.
Next row: K3, p to last 3 sts, k3.
Rep the last 2 rows 3 times more.
Change to 3¾ mm (UK 10/US 3) needles.
K 4 rows.
Cast off.

BACK

Work as given for front to **.

Next row: K11, turn.

Next row: K2, p to end.

Next row: K11, turn.

Next row: K2, p to end.

Next row: K11, turn.

Next row: K2, p to last 3 sts, k3.

Rep the last 2 rows 3 times more.

Change to 3¼ mm (UK 10/US 3) needles.

K 4 rows.

Cast off.

With RS facing, rejoin yarn to rem sts.

Next row: K11.

Next row: P to last sts, k2.

Next row: K11.

Next row: P to last sts, k2.

Next row: K11.

Next row: K3, p to last 2 sts, k2.

Rep the last 2 rows 3 times more.

Change to 3¼ mm (UK 10/US 3) needles.

K 2 rows.

Buttonhole row: K1, yf, k2tog, k to end.

K 1 row.

Cast off.

Join shoulder seams, leaving 4 cm (1½ in) open for neck. Join side seams. Sew on button.

DUNGAREES

With 3¼ mm (UK 10/US 3) needles and Blue, cast on 40 sts.

K 3 rows.

Change to 4 mm (UK 8/US 6) needles.

Cont in st st.

Work 12 rows.

Cast on 6 sts at beg of next 2 rows. (52 sts.)

St st 26 rows.

Change to 3¼ mm (UK10/US 3) needles.

K 4 rows.

Cast off 36 sts, k to end. (16 sts.)

Change to 4 mm (UK 8/US 6) needles.

Next row: P to last 3 sts, k3.

Next row: K2, skpo, k to end.

Rep the last 2 rows 7 times more and first row again. (7 sts.)

Work 2 rows straight.

Change to 3¼ mm (UK 10/US 3) needles.

K 2 rows.

Buttonhole row: K2, yf, k2tog, k to end.

K 1 row.

Cast off.

Work a second leg to match, reversing all shapings.

STRAPS (make 2)

With 3¼ mm (UK 10/US 3) needles and Blue, cast on 4 sts.

Cont in g st until strap measures 22 cm (8½ in).

Cast off.

TO MAKE UP

Join centre front and centre back seams. Join inside leg seams. Attach one end of each strap to upper edge of back 2.5 cm (1 in) from centre seam. Attach buttons securely to other ends of straps.

Clown

This colourful clown is sure to provide lots of fun and amusement with his cheery colours, smiling face, and big red nose.

SKILL LEVEL 3

MEASUREMENTS
Approximately 41 cm (16 in) high

MATERIALS
- 2 x 50 g balls of Rowan Handknit DK Cotton in each of Pale Pink and Yellow
- 1 x 50 g ball of Rowan Handknit DK Cotton in each of White, Red, Blue, Green and Orange
- Pair of 3¼ mm (UK 10/US 3), 3¾ mm (UK 9/US 5) and 4 mm (UK 8/US 6) knitting needles
- Washable toy stuffing
- 3.25 mm (UK 10/US 3) crochet hook

ABBREVIATIONS
See page 14.

TENSION
22 sts and 30 rows to 10 cm (4 in) measured over stocking stitch using 3¾ mm (UK 9/US 5) needles.

DOLL
BACK
With 3¾ mm (UK 9/US 5) needles and Pale Pink, cast on 35 sts.
Beg with a k row, work 40 rows in st st.
Mark each end of last row with a coloured thread.
** Work a further 49 rows.
Next row: P16, cast off next 3 sts, p to end.
Cont in stripes of 4 rows White and 4 rows Orange.
Cont on last set of sts for first leg.
Work 40 rows in st st.
Mark each end of last row. **
Cont in White only.
Work 6 rows.
Shape Heel
Next row: K8, skpo, k1, turn.
Next row: P2, p2tog, p1, turn.

Next row: K3, skpo, k1, turn.
Next row: P4, p2tog, p1, turn.
Cont in this way, dec one st as set on every row until 10 sts rem, ending with a p row.
Leave these sts on a holder.
Beg with 4 rows White, now cont in stripes of 4 rows Orange and 4 rows White.
With right side facing and beg at marker, pick up and k 6 sts from side of heel, k10 sts from holder, pick up and k 6 sts from other side of heel to marker. (22 sts.)
Cont in st st, dec one st at each end of 3 foll 4th rows. (16 sts.)
Work 11 rows, ending with 4 rows Orange.
Shape Toes
*** Cont in White only.
Next row: K1, skpo, k to last 3 sts, k2tog, k1.
P 1 row.
Rep last 2 rows once more. (12 sts.)
K 1 row.
Next 2 rows: P9, turn, k to end.
Next 2 rows: P6, turn, k to end. ***
Leave these sts on a spare needle.
With right side facing, rejoin yarn to rem sts for second leg and work as given for first leg, reversing shaping.

FRONT
With 3¾ mm (UK 9/US 5) needles and Pale Pink, cast on 35 sts.
Beg with a k row, work 22 rows in st st.
Next row: K12 in Pale Pink, 11 White, 12 Pale Pink.
Next row: P10 in Pale Pink, 15 White, 10 Pale Pink.
Next row: K8 in Pale Pink, 19 White, 8 Pale Pink.
Next row: P7 in Pale Pink, 21 White, 7 Pale Pink.
Next row: K6 in Pale Pink, 23 White, 6 Pale Pink.
Next row: P6 in Pale Pink, 23 White, 6 Pale Pink.
Rep the last 2 rows five times more.
Next row: Using Pale Pink, K to end.
Next row: Using Pale Pink, P to end.
Mark each end of last row with a coloured thread.

Work as given for Back from ** to **.
Work a further 24 rows in st st.

Shape Toes

Work as given from Back to *** to ***.

With right sides of back and front together and taking 1 st from each needle and working them tog, cast off toe sts.

With right side facing, rejoin yarn to rem sts for second leg and complete as given for first leg, reversing toe shaping.

ARMS (make 2)

With 3¾ mm (UK 9/US 5) needles and Pale Pink, cast on 26 sts.
Beg with a k row work 34 rows in st st.
Shape thumb.

Next row: K13, m1, k13.
P 1 row.
Next row: K13, m1, k1, m1, k13.
P 1 row.
Next row: K13, m1, k3, m1, k13.
P 1 row.
Next row: K13, m1, k5, m1, k13. (33 sts.)
P 1 row.
Next row: K20, turn and cast on one st.
Next row: P8, turn and cast on one st.
Work 4 rows on these 9 sts.
Next row: K1, [k2tog] 4 times.
Break yarn, thread through rem sts, pull up, fasten off securely, then join thumb seam.
With right side facing, rejoin yarn at base of thumb, pick up and k 2 sts from base of thumb, k to end. (28 sts.)
Work 9 rows.

Shape top

Next row: Skpo, k10, k2tog, skpo, k10, k2tog.
Next row: P to end.
Next row: Skpo, k8, k2tog, skpo, k8, k2tog.
Next row: P to end.
Next row: Skpo, k6, k2tog, skpo, k6, k2tog. (16 sts.)
Next row: P8, turn.
With right sides together, fold arm in half, taking 1 st from each needle and working them together, cast off.

NOSE

With 3¼ mm (UK 10/US 3) needles and Red, cast on 14 sts.
Beg with a k row, cont in st st.
Work 2 rows.
Next row: K1, * m1, k1; rep from * to end. (27 sts.)
Work 5 rows.
Next row: * K1, k2tog; rep from * to end. (18 sts.)
P 1 row.
Next row: * k2tog; rep from * to end.
Next row: P1, *p2tog; rep from * to end.
Thread yarn through rem sts, pull up and fasten off securely.
Join seam.

HAIR

Using Yellow, make a selection of twisted cords 6–12 cm (2½–5 in) long (see page 13).

TO MAKE UP

Join back and front together, leaving cast-on edge free. Stuff firmly.

Thread a length of yarn round neck edge between markers, pull up tightly and fasten off securely.

Knot approximately 24 hair cords through cast-on edge of head.

Stuff head, gather cast-on edge, pull up and secure, join gathers to form a seam across top of head. Knot remaining hair cords around top of head.

Stuff nose lightly and sew in position.

Join arm seams, leaving end open, stuff firmly and close opening.

Sew to side seams of body.

Using Blue, embroider eyes in satin stitch. Using Red, embroider mouth in stem stitch.

JUMPER
BACK & FRONT ALIKE

With 3¾ mm (UK 9/US 5) needles and Blue, cast on 44 sts.

K3 rows.

Cont in st st stripes of 2 rows Yellow, Red, Green, Blue; these 8 rows form patt, rep throughout until 38 rows have been worked.

Change to blue, k 5 rows. Cast off.

SLEEVES

With 3¾ mm (UK 9/US 5) needles and Blue, cast on 40 sts.

K3 rows.

Cont in st st stripes as set for Back and Front. Rep throughout until 24 rows have been worked. Cast off.

TO MAKE UP

Join 5 cm (2 in) from each end for shoulders. Sew on sleeves. Join side and sleeve seams.

TROUSERS (make 2 pieces)

With 3¾ mm (UK 9/US 5) needles and Yellow, cast on 58 sts. K 3 rows.

Work in st st patt using Yellow and Blue from Chart on page 108 to end of row 39.

Using Yellow, k 3 rows.

Cast off.

Straps

With 3¾ mm (UK 9/US 5) needles and Yellow, cast on 5 sts.

Cont in g st until strap measures 18 cm (7 in).

Cast off.

☐ Yellow

● Blue

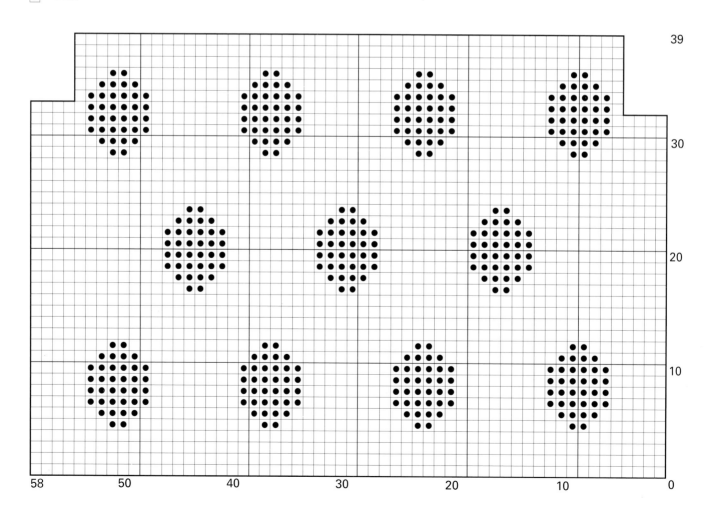

TO MAKE UP

Join inner leg seams. Join front and back seam. Sew straps in place.

BOW

With 3¾ mm (UK 9/US 5) needles and Red, cast on 7 sts.
Cont in g st until bow measures 25 cm (10 in).
Cast off.

Centre

With 4 mm (UK 8/US 6) needles and Red, cast on 10 sts.
K 10 rows.
Cast off.

TO MAKE UP

Join cast-on and cast-off ends of bow together.
With seam at centre back, wrap centre round centre of bow and join row end edges together.
Sew bow to neckband of jumper at centre front.

SHOES

With 3¾ mm (UK 9/US 5) needles and Blue, cast on 40 sts.
K 1 row.
Inc row: P twice in first st, p18, p twice in each of next 2 sts, p18, p twice in last st.
K 1 row.
Inc row: P twice in first st, p20, p twice in each of next 2 sts, p20, p twice in last st.
K 1 row.
Inc row: P twice in first st, p22, p twice in each of next 2 sts, p22, p twice in last st.

K 1 row. (52 sts.)
Work 5 rows in st st.
Shape instep
Next row: K30, skpo, turn.
Next row: P9, p2tog, turn.
Next row: K9, skpo, turn.
Rep the last 2 rows 7 times more, then the first of the 2 rows again.
Next row: K to end. (34 sts.)
Work 8 rows st st.
K 1 row.
Cast off.
Join back heel and sole seam.
Using Red make 2 twisted cords 40 cm (16 in) long and thread through shoe to tie at front.

HAT

With 3¾ mm needles (UK 9/US 5) and Blue, cast on 81 sts.
Work 8 rows st st.
Now work in stripe patt as follows:
Cont in stripes of 2 rows Red, Green, Yellow, Orange, Blue; these 10 rows form patt, rep throughout until 12 rows have been worked.
Shape Crown
1st row: K1, * k2tog, k6; rep from * to end. (71 sts.)
P 1 row.
3rd row: K1, * k2tog, k5; rep from * to end. (61 sts.)
P 1 row.
5th row: K1, *k2tog, k4; rep from * to end. (51 sts.)
P 1 row.
7th row: K1, * k2tog, k3; rep from * to end. (41 sts.)
P 1 row.
9th row: K1, * k2tog, k2; rep from * to end. (31 sts.)
P 1 row.
11th row: K1, * k2tog, k1; rep from * to end. (21 sts.)
P 1 row.
13th row: K1, * k2tog; rep from * to end. (11 sts.)
Break yarn, thread through rem sts, pull up tightly and fasten off securely.

TO MAKE UP

Join Back seam. Reversing seam on first 6 rows.

Suppliers

Most large department stores carry a good range of knitting yarns and accessories. Look in the Yellow Pages under Knitting Wool Suppliers.

UK

Bobbins
Wesley Hall
Church Street
Whitby
North Yorkshire
YO22 4DE
Tel: (01947) 600585
Mail order available

Bow Peep
36 Liverpool Road
Longton, Preston
Lancashire
PR4 5AU
Tel: (01772) 614508
Knitting yarns from all the major manufacturers

C&H Fabrics
8 High Street
Winchester
Hampshire
SO23 9JX
Tel: (01962) 843355
Fax: (01962) 829928
Email candhwinchester@talk21.com
www.candh.demon.co.uk
Stocks yarns from the major wool manufacturers. Branches in Brighton, Canterbury, Chichester, Eastbourne, Maidstone and Tunbridge Wells

Creative Crafts
47 Station Rd
Sheringham
Norfolk
NR26 8RG
Tel: (01263) 823153

David Morgan
26 The Hayes
Cardiff
Wales
CF10 1UG
Tel: (029) 2022 1011
Stocks a range of knitting yarns

Jaeger Handknits
Green Lane Mill
Holmfirth
West Yorkshire
HD9 2DX
Tel: (01484) 680050
Call for details of your nearest stockist

Jenners Ltd
48 Princes Street
Edinburgh
Midlothian
EH2 2YJ
Tel: (0131) 225 2442
Mail order available

John Lewis
Oxford Street
London
W1A 1EX
Tel: (020) 7629 7711
www.johnlewis.com
Stocks a wide range of yarns

Liberty
214 Regent Street
London
W1R 6AH
Tel: (020) 7734 1234
Stockists of a wide range of yarns. Mail order available

Patons Yarns
Tel: (01325) 394241
Email: consumer.ccuk@coats.com
Call the customer helpline for details of your nearest stockist

Rowan Yarns
Green Lane Mill
Holmfirth
West Yorkshire
HD9 2DX
Tel: (01484) 681881
Fax: (01484) 687920
www.knitrowan.com
Worldwide distribution. Call for details of your nearest stockist

Truro Fabrics
105-106 Kenwyn Street
Truro
Cornwall
TR1 3BX
Tel: (01872) 222130
www.trurofabrics.com
Mail order service available

SOUTH AFRICA

ABC Knitting & Haberdashery
327 President Street
Germiston 1401
Tel: (011) 873 4296

Brooklyn Wool Shop
Duncan Street
Pretoria
Tel: (012) 464 504

The Image
23 Lynwood Shopping Centre
Lynwood Road
Lynwood Ridge
Pretoria 0081
Tel: (012) 361 1737

Knitting Nook
5 Library Lane
Somerset West
Cape Town 7130
Tel: (021) 852 3044

Knitting Wool Centre (Pty) Ltd
122 Victoria Road
Woodstock
Cape Town 7025
Tel: (021) 447 1134

Orion Wool Shop and
Needlecraft
39 Adderley Street
Cape Town 8000
Tel: (021) 461 6941

Swansdown Knitting Wools
8 Foundry Lane
Durban 4001
Tel: (031) 304 0488

Trienies
Shop 41, Sanlam Centre
Leraatsfontein
Witbank 1034
Tel: (013) 692 4196

AUSTRALIA

Greta's Handcraft Centre
321 Pacific Highway
Lindfield
NSW 2070
Tel: (02) 9416 2489
*Carry a large range of Rowan Yarns and
can give further information on stockists*

Knitters of Australia
498 Hampton Street
Hampton
VIC 3188
Tel: (03) 9533 1233

Lincraft
Imperial Arcade
Pitt Street
Sydney
NSW 2000
Tel: (02) 9221 5111
www.lincraft.com.au

Sunspun
185 Canterbury Road
Canterbury
VIC 3126
Tel: (03) 9830 1609

NEW ZEALAND

Knit World
Selected branches stock Rowan
wools, phone first to find out.
Branches nationwide:
Auckland – (09) 837 6111
Tauranga – (07) 577 0797
Hastings – (06) 878 0090
New Plymouth – (06) 758 3171
Palmerston North – (06) 356 8974
Wellington – (04) 385 1918
Christchurch – (03) 379 2300
Dunedin – (03) 477 0400

Spotlight Stores
Branches throughout New Zealand
www.spotlightonline.co.nz
Manukau - Tel: (09) 263 6760
    or 0800 162 373
Wairau Park - Tel: (09) 444 0220
    or 0800 224 123
Hamilton - Tel: (07) 839 1793
New Plymouth - Tel: (06) 757 3575
Wellington - Tel: (04) 472 5600
Christchurch - Tel: (03) 377 6121

Woolmart Wools
Branches throughout South Island
and Auckland
*Check listings in your local white or
Yellow Pages (under "Knitting Wool")*

www.thewoolcompany.com

Acknowledgments

My special thanks go to all my family, especially Lucy and Molly.

My thanks also to the following:
everyone at Rowan Yarns; all the brilliant knitters: Tina Church, Rae Fraser, Linda Wood and Margaret Sperring; Tina Egleton; Penny Hill and Tina Church for making my toys come alive; Sue Whiting for her expert pattern checking; Shona Wood for her beautiful photography; Lisa Tai, the book designer. Finally I would like to thank Clare Sayer and Rosemary Wilkinson for all their hard work and support and for making this book possible.

Index